TELL IT LIKE A TOPGUN

TELL IT LIKE A TOPGUN

CREATE
WEAPONS SCHOOL WORTHY
PRESENTATIONS

JEFF "GOLDY" GOLDFINGER
US NAVAL AVIATION WEAPONS SCHOOL INSTRUCTOR

ENDORSEMENTS

"Goldy's *Tell It Like A TOPGUN* provides an invaluable insight into TOPGUN's biggest asset—how it develops instructors who can effectively teach and present complex material. Writing from experience, Goldy delves into all of the key attributes that make a presenter truly top-notch and shows the reader how to apply each to any type of speaking opportunity, so that everyone has the chance to *Tell It Like A TOPGUN.* It is a must-have book for anyone wanting to maximize their professional speaking proficiency."

~ **Brad Elward,** author of *TOPGUN: The Legacy—The Complete History of TOPGUN and Its Impact on Tactical Aviation*

"How can you capture the attention and affection of your customers and colleagues? Join former Navy tactics instructor Jeff "Goldy" Goldfinger as he translates military-style planning and execution into the world of business and professional presentations. Packed with powerful insights and step-by-step instructions, *Tell It Like a TOPGUN* brings you and those you serve into the bullseye of success together."

~ **Ron Kaufman,** *New York Times* bestselling author of *Uplifting Service*

"There is an art and science to effectively influencing others and "Goldy" weaves both into a how-to book that anyone who speaks to others should read. He lays out the steps you need to take to influence others and to see influence coming at you with memorable stories that will make you laugh out loud. It's the most enjoyable book on influence I have ever read."

~ **Paul Zak,** PhD, author of *Immersion: The Science of the Extraordinary and the Source of Happiness*

"As a former Naval Strike and Air Warfare instructor and combat fighter pilot, I can attest that Goldy has hit the oral presentation target with great precision here. As a former student learning aviation mishap investigation techniques from him at the Naval Postgraduate School, I know that Goldy practices what he preaches in his book. Even though his class subject wasn't overly interesting, his delivery made it both the most informative and memorable class. Even more relevant, as the former president of multiple billion-dollar businesses, personal and business success requires effective, communication and persuasion skills at all times. Goldy's recommendations are not only powerful for enhancing formal presentations but are essential life skills for success. An essential read."

~ **Todd Gautier,** Retired Fortune 250 President / Senior Exec, Former FA-18 Pilot and Weapons School Instructor

Published by Ink Heart Press

Paperback ISBN: 978-1-7380868-9-4

Hardcover ISBN: 978-1-0688442-1-8

Digital ISBN: 978-1-0688442-0-1

DEDICATION

To my wife Yeiry, for her unwavering support and to the memory of "Doc" Brown who still inspires me, 20-plus years after his passing.

FOREWORD 1

It's been my pleasure to know Jeff "Goldy" Goldfinger since 1999 when we both served at the Naval Strike and Air Warfare Center in Fallon, Nevada. At the time, Goldy was the subject matter expert on the tactical use of unmanned aerial vehicles, a new focus area and capability. I was the Director of Training with oversight of the team charged with preparing Navy Carrier air wings for deployment and potential combat operations. I was also in charge of the Navy Fighter Weapons School, or TOPGUN. TOPGUN's charter then as now, was to train the trainers, Strike Fighter Tactics Instructors, who eventually train and standardize their squadron and air wing aircrew on the latest tactics to win in combat.

TOPGUN instructors are known for their skill and perfection at delivering world class and expert subject matter presentations. Each instructor literally spends hundreds of hours researching, designing, practicing, and perfecting the delivery of their presentation to peers before ever presenting it to a TOPGUN class. There is nothing else like it in the United States Navy and it is the backbone of what makes the Navy Fighter Weapons School the premier graduate level aviation training program in the world. This model of preparing and perfecting presentations has been replicated by the instructors at other naval aviation weapons schools. The ability to stand up in front of a classroom of skilled and knowledgeable military practitioners and make them even better through a well-researched, expertly designed, and skilled presentation is the foundation of naval aviation's effectiveness and success.

In the same light, well-crafted and skillfully delivered presentations are also the foundation of high consequence decision-making at the upper levels of the military and in the business world. I've observed time after time how "the presentation" makes the difference between success and failure when briefing or pitching an idea, solution, product, and/or proposed course of action to an admiral, general, CEO, or board of directors. Being able to design and deliver an effective presentation is the "secret sauce" and far more important than degrees and certificates and in some cases, experience and position.

Goldy's naval career uniquely focused on teaching and instructing during five tours of duty in a diverse array of subject areas, and at the undergraduate and graduate levels of naval aviation training. During this time, he honed his military instructor presentation skills to near perfection and developed a reputation as an expert on teaching and instructing. Goldy has spent his years after the Navy conducting in-depth research into applied, emerging neuroscience principles, to be able to explain why high-level teaching techniques, such as those found at TOPGUN, are so effective and well-received. A highly successful presentation coach and consultant, Goldy is uniquely qualified to lecture and write on this subject. *Tell it Like a TOPGUN* reveals these high-level techniques to those in business, where the value of whatever advanced degrees and continuing education certificates they may have earned pales by comparison to the career potential they gain from standing up in front of a room full of their most qualified peers and delivering remarks. These presentations move the needle from improving sales, correcting broken programs, and raising investment capital, to briefing boards and shareholders at annual meetings. In both the TOPGUN and business environments, having the ability to articulate effectively at the highest levels is more than combat or career survival, it is literally how the utmost levels of personal and organizational success are achieved. Goldy wants to share what he knows and has developed, to support our next generation in achieving career success in whatever field they are in.

Being able to design and deliver a compelling presentation when it really counts is an acquired skill that takes time and work. It is also a critical skill set necessary to fulfill one's potential and absolutely essential for rising to the top echelons of any organization. *Tell it Like a TOPGUN* has the secrets to producing compelling presentations via a logical and in-depth step-by-step process. The book delivers the what and the how to design and deliver a winning presentation. It also presents the science behind each step to enable the reader to understand and appreciate the context and importance of each step of Goldy's process. It is full of examples and can be applied to any presentation to make it world class. *Tell it Like a TOPGUN* is a must read for all presenters. I've read it cover to cover and it has immediately helped me improve my presentation skills and will be a valued addition and resource in the personal library of any aspiring or established professional. Regardless of your experience and position, *Tell it Like a TOPGUN* will improve your ability to design and give highly compelling presentations when they count the most.

W.G. (Bill) Sizemore II, Rear Admiral, US Navy (Ret.)

FOREWORD 2

This original work is an invaluable asset and resource for yourself and your entire company.

If you are interested in improving your sales, marketing, and overall communication skills then this book is an absolute must have. *There is simply not another book like this on the market. Period.* As a TOPGUN graduate and former CEO myself, I can personally attest to the value and uniqueness of Goldy's approach. This bringing together of science...especially how the brain processes information and how we humans make decisions... with serious rigor in the discipline of making useful, actionable decisions, makes *Tell It Like a TOPGUN* an original and invaluable resource. Add in full measures of humor and wit, and you have a go-to manual like no other. From practical guidance of Tactics, Techniques, and Procedures (TTPs), to effective methods of presentation, to education on phenomena like the "forgetting curve", this work is fascinating, easy to read, and understandable.

As the CEO of a defense company, I brought Goldy's in-person training to the top people in our company and it made a tangible and significant difference. This was not only exceptionally valuable for those in direct contact with our customers, but for all those in the C-suite, and those who were VPs and team leaders in all disciplines (engineers, program managers, et al.) as well. I would do it again, and I strongly recommend you make the investment that this outstanding book provides to improving yourself and your workforce.

Anyone interested in taking communication skills to the highest level will benefit from this outstanding and altogether unique blend of science and experience. *Tell it like a TOPGUN* is your opportunity to take advantage of the techniques perfected and honed at the Navy Fighter Weapons School over decades of disciplined attention to every detail, and to capitalize on Goldy's study of neuroeconomics. I predict you will find yourself buying copies for your fellow leaders, subordinates, and associates at many levels in your organization.

Dan Donoghue, Commander, US Navy (retired)
and Former CEO, Ravenswood Solutions

AUTHOR'S NOTE

I attended a very prestigious, globally ranked university as an undergraduate, where I noticed that brilliant, renowned professors aren't natural-born teachers. In fact, to become a university professor rarely, if ever, requires learning how to teach adult learners. By contrast, becoming an instructor at the US Navy Fighter Weapons School (a.k.a. TOPGUN) requires many months of preparation and peer evaluation before one can be certified to teach.

The "Bros in Blue" (TOPGUN instructors call themselves Bros and they always wear a light blue t-shirt under their flight suits) have a half-century-long history of superior instructional design and execution. Fortunately for the rest of naval aviation, their methodology has been adopted by every one of the other four aviation weapons schools. It was while I was an instructor at two of those other schools that I was privileged to learn what retired 4-star Admiral "Rat" Willard, a former TOPGUN instructor, so admiringly describes.

> Anybody who has spent time at [the] Navy Fighter Weapons School in the past fifty years would immediately comment on two things: the absolute professionalism of its instructors and the total precision of its instruction, whether in the classroom or in the air.[1]

Nearly a decade ago, when I started developing the workshop and student manual that evolved into this book, I sampled the marketplace for presentation skills training courses and noticed three themes. First, nearly all the programs were (and perhaps still are) divided into two camps—teaching the design of your deck or learning delivery techniques. Second, whether design- or delivery-centric, they were the educational equivalent of undergraduate-level instruction, for those with little or no existing skills. I could count on one hand the number of TOPGUN worthy instructional programs that are so crucial to business survival. Lastly, due to limited time and a desire to make it widely available at low cost, the programs restricted their content to the ***how*** and ***what*** to do, omitting the ***why*** it worked.

---

1 Brad Elward, TOPGUN: *The legacy: The complete history of TOPGUN and its impact on tactical aviation* (Schiffer Publishing, 2021), 15.

For casual, everyday presentations, the undergrad approach is a perfectly acceptable skills acquisition strategy. But, someday soon, you'll be required to deliver a presentation that puts the survival of your product, business, or career at stake. For that, you need to *Tell It Like a TOPGUN.*

My conclusions lead to the creation of my 3-day workshop, which has now had hundreds of graduates, and its accompanying student notetaking manual, the impetus for this book. While you can certainly read this book as a standalone, hopefully entertaining treatise on the topic, my recommendation is that, while reading, you imagine being in class with me while you design and rehearse the delivery of your own, highly consequential presentation.

PREFACE

Welcome to public speaking—the world's second oldest profession.

Growing up in West Orange, New Jersey (exit 145 on the Parkway, for any fellow Jerseyans reading this), I was the classic "Big Bang Theory" geek with a telescope, a basement chemistry lab, and an Erector Set. Our town's only claim to fame was as the home and second lab of the famous inventor Thomas Edison.

Joining the US Navy to fly on and off aircraft carriers was the furthest thing from my parents' minds when they sent me off to a highly selective, well known university to earn an engineering degree. While it disturbed them that I had joined the Naval Reserve Officer Training Corps (NROTC) in my freshman year, they probably thought I'd grow out of it like a young boy who briefly falls in love with the "bad girl" from the other side of town.

Imagine their shock when at the start of my junior year I signed the Navy's "marriage proposal" (contract) committing me to serve at least four years after graduation. My genetic profile says that I am 99.7% Ashkenazi Jew. I suppose my parents blamed the other 0.3% for driving me into the arms of the Navy.

A 1980s era advertising slogan for the Navy promised, "It's not just a job. It's an adventure." I couldn't have said it better myself. After graduation, I spent the next twenty years flying high performance military aircraft, visited 25 countries, instructed thousands of my colleagues in essential combat tactics, techniques, and procedures (TTPs in Navy jargon), and safe flying best practices, and listening to some of the most awe-inspiring leadership speeches.

But the childhood geek in me still resonated with two of Edison's inventions that would serve me best in my career as a public speaker—the phonograph (the predecessor to compact discs) and Black Maria (his motion picture studio that produced over 1,200 films). Why those two?

Once he invented the incandescent light bulb, the technology didn't change much over time. You would be hard-pressed to look at such a bulb today, in the sea of LED bulbs, compare it to a lightbulb from 1890, and see much difference.

The phonograph was a different matter. The first was made from tinfoil wrapped around a cylinder. The recording could only be played back a few times before it wore out. But over time, several design improvements appeared as tinfoil morphed into wax, the cylinder became a disc, the discs could be played back infinitely, and they came in multiple sizes and playback speeds (first 78 rpm, then 33 and later the ubiquitous 45 single).

My takeaway? Whatever you're producing, always be looking for ways to improve it.

Black Maria caught my attention because of the rollers. The studio was built on wheels that rolled around a circular track with a roof that could be popped open like an observatory's protective dome. The purpose of the wheels and the pop-top lid was to allow sunlight to stream in from every angle. Think about this for a minute. The man that invented indoor lighting had to find a solution to harness a more powerful light for his storytelling.

My takeaway? Do whatever it takes to fully immerse your audience.

You'll see these Edison-inspired influences in this book. I'll often reference pop culture movies and songs, and how each art form is able to tell emotionally gripping stories, a key component to producing the most memorable and actionable presentations. From Meatloaf's groundbreaking musical ballad "Paradise by the Dashboard Light" to Sylvester Stallone's *Rocky* (a movie that made 235x its budget at the box office), we humans love great storytelling no matter the medium.

Anyway, I joined the NROTC program two weeks before the start of my freshman year, mostly out of curiosity. The ROTC military staff had two members with combat experience from the horrific Vietnam conflict—Marine Gunnery Sergeant Poyner and our Commanding Officer, Navy Captain Kenneth Coskey. Gunny was a Marine's Marine (think R. Lee Ermey's Gunny Hartman character in the movie Full Metal Jacket). The Skipper was an aviator shot down over enemy territory and spent more than five years at the infamous Hỏa Lò Prison, which was given the dark humor nickname "The Hanoi Hilton" by prisoner of war Robert Shumaker.

Between the Gunny and the Skipper, I heard many stories of brotherhood, teamwork, survival, and, most prominently, respect for the distinction between the military's creed to follow orders and the source of those directives—elected politicians. Of course, I recognized the subtle indoctrination I was subjected to. It worked. I remained in ROTC throughout college and spent the next twenty years willingly serving. And I got to do some outrageously cool things along the way. I flew as a crewman in nearly twenty types of aircraft from the T-2 Buckeye jet trainer to the Mach 2 capable F-14 Tomcat. I served in three "wars" (Cold War, Gulf War, Drug War), drank a lot of adult beverages in seedy overseas bars, ate many unknown street foods, and, just in case I ever run for public office, I never, ever stored classified materials in boxes at my house.

My Navy career is only one aspect of my journey to professional public speaking. It started much earlier. While in college, I became a certified Water Safety Instructor with the American Red Cross. The summer of my senior year I took a job as the waterfront director at a summer camp in the Wisconsin Dells, a popular vacation destination in middle America where mosquitoes are considered the state bird. I led a team of water sports instructors responsible for all swim, ski, and sailing instruction. At the time, Camp Chi was located on a small lake that was about an eighth of a mile wide by half-a-mile long. The camp's swim area was roped off like you would see in any movie about summer camp (think Ivan Reitman's *Meatballs* with Bill Murray). For their own safety, we explained to the gullible pre-teens that another "Loch Ness monster" lived outside the rope so they wouldn't ever swim there.

At the end of the summer, we had the traditional graduation swim which allowed everyone to cross the width of the lake on their own. I'll never forget the look on one young swimmer's face as she approached the halfway mark. With a jitter in her voice and even less control over her swim stroke, she called out to me in the safety boat:

"Mr. G.! Mr. G.! I can't make it. Can I please get in the boat?"

I had seen her swim all summer long and knew she could finish. She had merely lost her confidence. If you're a coach, then you already know how you would've handled this. Instead of enabling her defeatism by pulling her into the safety boat, I slipped into the water and swam alongside using a calm voice to help her restore her strength and determination. I climbed back into the boat and, some minutes later, watched with pride as her four-foot something frame met the opposite shoreline whereupon she stood up, turned around, and looked at me with arms held high and an ear-to-ear beaming smile as if she'd just scored the match point at Wimbledon.

As proud as she was of her own accomplishment, I was just as proud of mine for not letting her quit when it got hard. Right there, I realized my mission in life was to help others swim across whatever they happen to call their lake. That's the impetus for my life as an educator and now, this book.

While a Naval officer, I managed to finagle my way into five instructor tours—three weapons school tours, the E-2 Hawkeye training squadron, and the Naval Postgraduate School. Add to that the hundreds of pre-mission flight briefings and post-mission debriefs, and you can quickly conclude that I've spent thousands of hours prepping and delivering high consequence oral presentations.

But that's just the military component. While attending Navy flight school in Pensacola, Florida, I taught a night school computer class at the local junior college (now renamed Pensacola State College). Then, while living in San Diego, when I was stationed at the now famous Miramar Naval Air Station, setting of the original 1986 *Top Gun* movie, I became certified by the Red Cross as both a First Aid and CPR Instructor and then as an Instructor Trainer. This adds many more hundreds of hours and students to my portfolio.

In total, for the past four decades, both in and out of uniform, I have spoken at conferences, workshops, and webinars worldwide, for audiences from 1 to 1,000. In other words, I have accumulated well above Malcolm Gladwell's 10,000 hours[2] and I feel unapologetic in claiming a certain level of public speaking mastery.

Most fortunately, 32 years after that little girl swam across that Wisconsin lake, I was able to turn my personal mission into a profitable, self-employed business. That doesn't mean it has always been easy, comfortable, or standing ovation worthy. It means that I can share the accumulated experiences, good and not-so, from decades of public speaking to help you swim across your own public speaking lake.

As you move through this book, I'll share some of my most meaningful accomplishments. Like the time I coached two "hardcore" engineers to give a presentation in front of a product selection committee that eventually awarded their company (my client) a $250-million contract. As a consultant hired to help them write their response to a competitive Request for Proposal (RFP), they were then down selected from a large pool of candidate companies to give an oral presentation in front of the selection

2 Malcolm Gladwell, Outliers: *The story of success* (Little, Brown, 2008).

board. I spent five days successfully coaching them in how to *Tell It Like a TOPGUN*, the same method you'll learn here.

Finally, one of the compliments I frequently receive is about my ability to tell engaging stories. So much so that one of my friends who has heard many of them would officially christen a session by announcing, "It's now story time with Goldy." So, I'll be sprinkling that phrase throughout the book at strategic locations to drive home a particular learning objective.

TABLE OF CONTENTS

COMMANDER'S INTENT

PART 1: MISSION PLANNING

PART 2: MISSION EXECUTION

PART 3: MISSION ADMIN

COMMANDER'S INTENT

INTRODUCTION

According to most studies, people's number one fear is public speaking. Number two is death. Death is number two! Does that sound right? This means to the average person, if you go to a funeral, you're better off in the casket than doing the eulogy.

~ Comedian Jerry Seinfeld

A DAY THAT WILL LIVE IN INFAMY

On February 1, 2003, I was sitting in the bleachers at Kennedy Space Center, Florida, waiting for the Space Shuttle Columbia to land. Onboard was my BFF, Navy Captain David Brown, Mission Specialist. As you might know, it was not to be as his spacecraft disintegrated upon reentry killing all seven crewmembers.

Six weeks later, I was asked to deliver his eulogy at Arlington National Cemetery. At that point in my career, I was already a highly accomplished speaker. I had overcome stage fright, as one of those rare individuals that learned to enjoy speaking in front of an audience.

This very public speech was different. This was no ordinary funeral, as if there ever is such a thing. Given the media attention, expansiveness of the attendee list, and my grief, I struggled to find the courage for days to begin the eulogy delivery design process.

The delivery day finally arrived. March 12, 2003, the Old Post Chapel.

As I walked to the pulpit in my Navy Blues (our most formal uniform), I passed by the closed casket. Any remaining fear of public speaking emerged deep inside my psyche. It finally felt real. I choked up inside. Me, the 1s and 0s geek, fluid starting to leak from my eyeballs like everyone else.

So, stepping to the podium, I took out a stack of 8½ x 11-inch papers, inhaled deeply…and opened with a joke.

"In asking me to give one of the eulogies, Dave's father cautioned me that Arlington has a tightly choreographed process and that I needed to keep my remarks under five minutes."

I folded the papers in half, tucked them in my right-hand breast pocket, then reached into my left-hand breast pocket and pulled out a few 3 x 5 index cards.

"So, this morning, I went to the hotel's business center and shrunk my speech on the copier."

His parents and brother smiled and nodded their heads approvingly. The rest of the attendees chuckled quietly.

My purposes for opening with this story are threefold. First, I want you to realize that even the most highly-accomplished public speakers and personalities are just as scared as I was that day—professor, motivational speaker, author Brené Brown and singer, actor, director Barbra Streisand being two widely-known examples.

Second, this story reinforces that public speaking is never about what you want to say, rather it's about what the audience wants and needs to hear.

Third, even if you enjoy public speaking, the laborious crafting and editing process of a consequential presentation is often looked upon with dread, like the weeks spent cleaning and staging your house prior to presenting it for sale. While I abhorred losing my BFF, I found immense pleasure in the loving effort to give life to a few words about his death.

I have included the full speech in Part 3f and encourage you to read it twice. Once now, while the story is fresh in your mind. Then, later, after I share the underlying tactics, techniques, and procedures (TTPs) that allowed me to craft such a memorable narrative. Read it as if doing a frog dissection in science class to make the academic practical. (I have included line numbers in the speech so that I can easily reference individual TTPs back to specific parts of the speech.)

NAVIGATING OUR MISSION TOGETHER

As I write this, *Top Gun: Maverick* approaches $1.5 billion at the box office. While the idea for this book and its title have been with me for years, I am unapologetically taking advantage of this pop culture publishing opportunity to attract a larger audience. Not just to increase book sales, but because I believe in my message strongly enough to ride the wave.The endorsers of *Tell It Like a TOPGUN* (or *TILT*) and I are convinced that great oral presentation skills are as vital to having a successful career as breathing is to survival. This is also supported in scientific research.

The most striking parts of both the original movie and its sequel focus on the precision flying scenes. Those are the adrenaline-pumping, sensational sequences of both movies. However, most insiders will tell you that it's the classroom presence and discipline on the ground that truly distinguish a TOPGUN instructor from any number of shit hot pilots (Sierra Hotel in aviation lingo). That's the focus of this book—the Sierra Hotel knowledge, skills, and abilities required to stand in front of a room full of Mavericks and command their undivided attention.

Both *Top Gun* movies focused heavily on the high-intensity flight sequences with awe-inspiring visuals. While they hinted at the accompanying classroom portion of the syllabus, it was not made clear that for every hour spent in flying instruction, there are four or more hours of ground time in the classroom, pre-flight planning, and post-flight debriefing. I follow a similar path, where each chapter contains academics followed by instruction on how to immediately apply the learning to a specific stage in the development or delivery of your presentation.

For those that want to immediately start learning these new TTPs, you can dive right into Part 1 - Mission Planning (designing your presentation) followed by Part 2 – Mission Execution (delivery). However, I highly encourage you to finish the rest of this Commander's Intent part, then take a detour into Part 3 – Mission Admin where I provide the historical context for the real-life TOPGUN in the section titled The Weapons School Way. Only by understanding the combat-driven forcing function that led to its creation can you truly appreciate the gravitas of the organization, the staff, and the subsequent adoption of its methodology across the Navy's spectrum of sibling weapons schools. The rest of Part 3 is certainly useful (or I wouldn't have included it) but can wait until you complete Parts 1 and 2.

TILTING TOWARD WINDMILLS

To change your direction in an airplane, you don't turn the wheel. Instead, you tilt your wings in the direction you want to turn. This action causes the airplane's lift vector (the force that keeps an airplane in the air) to shift your flight's trajectory towards a new direction.

My purpose in writing this book was to teach you how to change your ***career trajectory*** by enhancing your oral presentation skills (your personal lift vector). For that reason, I want you to ***TILT*** in a new direction for design (Mission Planning) and delivery (Mission Execution).

And because we military types just loooove our acronyms, wouldn't you know it, TILT = Tell It Like a TOPGUN. Amazing how that worked out. Therefore, throughout the book, you will see me sprinkle **"TILT Angles"** as a "stomp the floor" reminder to change the direction of your thinking by employing the relevant TTP.

WARNING

If you TILT too little, you'll never reach your intended destination. If you TILT too much (overbanking, for the aviation purists), your aircraft can enter what is referred to as a "death spiral" where the lift vector causes an ever tightening turn and increasingly rapid descent. This is what happened to John F. Kennedy, Jr., in his Piper Saratoga in July 1999 during a routine pleasure flight. Therefore, regarding the TTPs I will teach you in this book, I warn you to TILT at just the right angle to achieve your business goals without harming your career identity.

"Good luck, Mr. Hunt."

WHAT'S HERE THAT YOU WON'T GET ELSEWHERE

In closing out this introduction, it's been almost a decade since a corporate client first asked me to develop a presentation skills course for their staff of engineers, scientists, and program managers. At the time, I knew the marketplace was flooded with such offers, so I wondered why this client didn't just pursue one of the myriad speaking programs on the market. They brought to my attention that their STEM-educated (science, technology, engineering, mathematics) employees had specific needs and goals when it came to presentations. These staffers typically presented design solutions to technical leads, gave product and service overviews to VIP visitors, made requests for development funding from government customers, or delivered talks at industry conferences. As I mentioned earlier, when I surveyed the landscape, I found there were plenty of workshops that focused on the design of the presentation (storyboarding, organization, and software tools), and others dedicated to delivery skills (posture, tone of voice, eye contact), but there were no training programs that combined both.

Furthermore, while the available training courses were (and still are) loaded with great ***what-to-do*** TTPs, they tend to be light on the ***why-it-works*** explanations. As former TOPGUN Commanding Officer "Pops" Papaioanu said: "Being on the staff requires an abnormal mixture of high talent, unrelenting passion, balanced humility, and an engineering mind."[3]

Being STEM-educated myself, I knew that my client's participants would want to know how to "engineer" their talk. To satisfy this need, I adopted a framework called neuroeconomics, the interdisciplinary field that includes:

- Neuroscience: how the brain is organized and functions
- Cognitive Psychology: our use of language and memory
- Behavioral Economics: decision-making under risk and uncertainty

Throughout the book, I have liberally sprinkled scientifically validated findings (the ***whys***) that justify my recommended TTPs (the ***whats***). One of the most frequent comments I receive in participant surveys is gratitude for including such fundamental knowledge as many of the students recognize how they can apply it to other aspects of both their professional and personal lives.

It's nine years since I delivered the first version of this workshop, originally titled and trademarked as ***Engineering the Talk***®. The material in this book and the accompanying workshop were previously only available to corporate clients whose staff were large enough to fill a room with at least fifteen participants. Dozens of iterations and hundreds of students later, this book benefits from the accumulation of all the classroom and

3 Elward, *TOPGUN,* 13.

execution lessons learned. As of February 2023, I have made my workshop available to the public (https://TellItLikeaTopgun.com to enroll) with this book included as a textbook for participants. Even if not enrolled in my workshop, I recommend you follow the sequence of lessons in this book as if you were.

MISSION DISTINCTIONS — SOME WORDS ABOUT WORDS

It's not what you say.
It's what they hear that counts.

~ Frank Luntz

CUSTOMERS, PROSPECTS, AND LISTENERS, OH MY

As a seller (of a product, service, or combat tactic) there are two types of buyers on the other side of the transaction: customers and prospects. By definition, a customer is someone who buys from us, while a prospect is a prospective customer who *may* buy from us *in the future*. I'll use the terms prospect, customer, and listener interchangeably throughout the book.

Notice above that I implied that buyers (customers, prospects, and listeners) are human beings. Former US presidential candidate Mitt Romney asserted on the campaign trail in 2011 that "corporations are people too." He might have been technically correct in the eyes of the law regarding taxes and legal rights, but I strongly discourage such an interpretation in the context of our work here.

A corporation doesn't sign a purchase order, approve your program plan, or request a demo of your product. A biological, linguistic, social human being does all those things. Sure, on behalf of a company, but that's not how you should prepare yourself. Rather, your listener's brain makes the decision to buy your product, service, or idea. If you take nothing else away from this book, I want you to remember that you're always presenting to fellow human beings first and foremost.

A ROAD TO ACTION: PART I

Next in line are a set of five specific words that are present in every presentation. Imagine a gathering of our pre-historic, hunter-gatherer ancestors when somebody came up with the bright idea (a.k.a. innovation) to kill a woolly mammoth. The leader of the attack had to give an oral presentation the night before that might have sounded something like this:

Mr. Slate: *Tomorrow we're going to kill a woolly mammoth.*

Fred Flintstone: *I don't think that's possible. We've never done it before and they're just too big.*

Mr. Slate: *I've seen it done by the tribe on the other side of the gravel pit. Barney Rubble and I are going to charge from the left flank. Wilma and Betty, the right flank. Bamm-Bamm and Pebbles will attack the rear while you, Fred, spear the beast right between its eyes. Are you all with me?!*

They cheer with excitement.

A few moments later, Barney comes up to Mr. Slate and has a private discussion.

Barney: *I don't think this is going to work, Mr. Slate. I've seen Fred throw a spear and he's terrible. He's my friend and all but with our lives on the line, my assessment is that he's not up to the task. However, I've been watching Wilma and I think she has both the accuracy and the calm-under-pressure style that's necessary for us to be successful.*

Mr. Slate: *Okay, Barney. I trust your judgment on this one. You've never let me down before.*

This hypothetical story of the Flintstone gang planning their first woolly mammoth kill is an example of how language produces action—what philosophers call Speech Acts,[4] words and phrases that not only convey information but cause the listener to perform a specific act.

The following exploration of the first 3 of 5 specific speech acts is based on the work of Dr. Fernando Flores[5] who claims these five "serve as a

---

4 https://en.wikipedia.org/wiki/Speech_act

5 Fernando Flores (author) and Maria Flores Letelier (editor), *Conversations for Action and Collected Essays: Instilling a culture of commitment in working relationships* (CreateSpace, 2012).

'periodic table' of the elements of coordination that is a generic and powerful foundation for design, no matter how complex the business process."[6]

ASSERTIONS

Assertions are factual claims that can be independently verified by a third-party observer as either true or false. Some examples include:

- The temperature outside today is 85°F.
- The train from London to Paris takes 2.5 hours.
- The cost to manufacture this part has decreased by 5% each year.
- Wilma has already killed three woolly mammoths this year with her spear.

These are assertions because we have a socially acceptable definition for each of the conditions. We all agree that the numerals 85 and 2.5 represent a specific quantity of worldwide standard Fahrenheit degrees and hours, respectively. We can agree on the definition of 5%, and we can count how many notches Wilma has carved onto her woolly mammoth-killing spear. Any third-party can test the veracity of the claim in each statement. If the claim is proven to be true, we interpret the speaker as being sincere—a person who tells an objective truth. If the claim is proven to be false, we label the speaker as a liar or, more appropriately, as a jerk for thinking we would fall for such a falsehood.

A few years ago, during the Donald Trump administration in the US, Rudy Giuliani (a Trump supporter) was being interviewed by a reporter regarding the details of something controversial. His response was: "You know, facts change over time." While his statement has some truth in it, I don't believe he meant it with the philosophical precision of a linguist. So let me further explore the notion of fact as a socially acceptable agreement.

For thousands of years, it was a factual assertion that the sun, moon, and planets revolved around the earth. That was until a few pesky philosophers from the 17th and 18th centuries (Nicolaus Copernicus and Galileo Galilei), plus a few more meddling mathematicians (Johannes Kepler and Isaac Newton), proved otherwise. The new heliocentric fact still took a couple

6 http://conversationsforaction.com/

of hundred years to be universally accepted. Other examples of facts that changed over time:

- Bloodletting is an acceptable medical treatment.
- The earth is flat.
- There's only one galaxy in the universe, ours.
- The moon is made of cheese.
- The Boston Red Sox will never win another World Series.

So, yes, Rudy, facts do change over time. But only when they can be independently verified and accepted by the vast majority. I say "vast" to account for "Flat Earthers" and those, like a close relative of mine, that don't believe the Apollo 11 astronauts landed on the moon in 1969. Nothing we can do there but to sigh and just say "bless their hearts."

So far, we have two types of speakers: the sincere and the liar/jerk. The third type of assertive speaker is the most dangerous—the bullshitter. Don't take my word for it. Princeton University's Professor Emeritus of Philosophy Harry Frankfurt said it best (and memorialized it in his iconic best seller[7]).

> The bullshitter is neither on the side of the true or the side of the false. His eye is not on the facts at all. He does not reject the authority of the truth, as the liar does, and opposes himself to it. He pays no attention to it at all. By virtue of this, bullshit is a greater enemy of the truth than lies are.

Hey, Rudy! Any comment?

My point in highlighting these three types of assertions—truthful, a lie, or bullshit—is the obvious caveat that weapons school instructors never, ever lie or bullshit our audience (except at a bar when we're trying to impress an unaccompanied member of the preferred sex). If an audience member asks a question that you don't know the answer to, admit your ignorance and, if appropriate, commit to getting back to them with the answer.

---

7 Harry G. Frankfurt. *On Bullshit* (Princeton University Press, 2019).

STORY TIME WITH GOLDY

Referring now to the eulogy (Part 3f), if you look at lines 1–4, you'll see I made some assertions about when and where I met Doc and what aircraft I was flying. Those are all independently verifiable by talking to my squadron mates. That makes me a sincere speaker.

Recap: Assertions are the first of the five fundamental speech acts in every presentation. Ensure all your assertions are verifiably true.

To make your presentation more credible, start making a list of assertions of fact you might want to include. Can they be independently verified as true?

ASSESSMENTS

Unlike assertions, assessments are neither true nor false. Rather, they're opinions of the assessor and are either "grounded" by factual observations or not—what might be termed an "ungrounded assessment" or more simply a "speculation."

Examples of assessments include:

- Goldy is a fantastic public speaker. You should hire him.
- Sara is a brilliant engineer. You should put her on your product team.
- Sam is a terrible coder. You shouldn't put him on your software team.
- Our company provides best-in-class customer service. You should buy our product.

Let's examine the grounding for each.

There is no universally accepted definition for "fantastic," "brilliant," "terrible," or "best-in-class." So we have two options: 1) make assumptions based on our own internal definitions, which invariably leads to the famous saying, "When you assume something it makes an 'ass' out of 'u' and 'me'" (ass + u + me = assume), or 2) press for the grounding.

"Why do you say, 'Goldy is a fantastic public speaker?'"

"Before we hired him, we looked at dozens of client testimonials that spoke to both the high quality of his content and the memorable style of his delivery. He didn't let us down. The comments we received after he delivered the keynote address at our corporate outing last month exceeded our expectations."

Clearly there's extensive, repeatable grounding for the assessment.

"Why do you say, 'Sara is a brilliant engineer?'"

"Well, she graduated with a 4.0 GPA, and we heard she has an IQ of 155."

Okay, that is certainly one form of grounding an assessment, although I'm not sure it will be helpful in the particular situation where Sara needs to perform in a real-world engineering role.

Consider, instead, if the conversation went something like this:

"Why do you say, 'Sara is a brilliant engineer?'"

"Well, that was the gossip about Sara before we hired her. She had worked at another company as an intern in college and when we checked up on her, that was the consensus opinion."

"Okay. And what about now?"

"In the last three product design meetings that she attended, each time the team was stuck on a particular issue, she was able to find an elegant solution that was easier to manufacture and had a higher reliability prediction."

"What about her GPA?"

"Oh, I don't really know what it is. Is that important to you?"

"I guess not. What about Sam? I heard some gossip that he's a terrible coder."

"Yeah, as his program manager, it really ticked me off that he was always showing up late or sometimes not at all to meetings. And when he did show up, he usually made side comments about unrelated matters that made it difficult for us to stay focused. He also tends to insult his teammates about their coding prowess which makes it harder for me to motivate the team to keep working with him."

"Oh, I see. Did he submit all his coding assignments on time?"

"Well, yes."

"Were his modules well-documented and error free?"

"Well, yes."

"Okay. So, if I put him on my project in a solo role that requires little coordination with others and not invite him to meetings, what would you say?"

"While I can't be certain because I don't have enough evidence. My speculation is that he'll do just fine."

"Great, thank you."

Notice that in each case, the assessment was based on the speaker's perspective of what was important to them. This is fair since there is no objective truth to an assessment. It is an opinion in someone else's frame of reference. As Einstein reminds us, everything's relative.

Did you notice not only the use of factual claims to back up the assessment but also that the fundamental purpose of an assessment is to notice the past to forecast and improve the future? In other words, opining for the sake of opining is almost as dangerous as spewing bullshit.

STORY TIME WITH GOLDY

Reading line 91 of the eulogy, "the humblest overachiever" is clearly an assessment since there's no universal definition of such a person. Throughout the speech, I kept giving assertions of both Doc's humility and accomplishments (e.g., Flight Surgeon of the Year, Dual Designator) which led me to opine that he was both humble and an overachiever.

TILT

Consider what assessments (e.g., opinions) you might want to share with your listeners. You may have grounding for forming these opinions to share.

DECLARATIONS

There's an old story about three baseball umpires sitting in a bar comparing notes about their craft. They were asked how they go about calling balls and strikes.

Umpire #1 replies: "I call 'em as I see 'em."

Umpire #2 says: "I call 'em as they are."

Umpire #3 offers: "They ain't nothin' 'til I call 'em."

The first umpire makes assessments of the strike zone, while the second claims an objective truth about his assertions of a strike. It's the third umpire that is the most interesting because the statement recognizes the true power of their authority to make declarations—the third type of speech act.

A declaration is neither an assertion nor an assessment. Rather, it brings forth something entirely new into existence.

For example:

- By the powers vested in me by the state of ________, I now declare you married. You may kiss your spouse.
- Our two companies are teamed up on this project.
- Our newest company product is called the Flux Capacitor.
- We're the world's leading manufacturer of flux capacitors.

In the first case, there's obviously no universal agreement on what it means to be married. You can't look at a couple and assess their marriage. Around the world there are at least six types of culturally acceptable marriages—straight, gay, monogamous, polygamist, polyamorous, and common law. But even within each marriage, couples decide for themselves the commitments (vows) they make as part of their declaration.

The plotline of the 2014 movie *5 to 7* involves an adulterous affair between a young writer (played by Anton Yelchin) in New York City and the wife of a French diplomat (Bérénice Lim Marlohe). The title comes from the accepted arrangement the wife has with her husband that allows them both to have extramarital lovers but only between the hours of 5 and 7 p.m. on weekdays and that each spouse shall meet and approve of the other's lover. It is a work of fiction and, perhaps, a condition you wouldn't accept in your own partnership but believable, nonetheless (ah, to be French). That is the central component of a declaration—they always come with vows that describe the future operating capabilities and constraints.

Later in the book, I'll highlight the power of humans to just make shit up as one of the abilities that helped us become the world's apex predator. It is here in this section, through declarations pulled from thin air, that reveal how we're able to do it.

"This is my cave and that's your cave." A declaration of ownership rights.

"This is a rock, this is a spear, that is a wheel, those are flux capacitors, that is an FA-18 Hornet." Product declarations are completely arbitrary. They too have vows, although we call them features, functions, and benefits instead.

When Steve Jobs announced the creation of the iPod, he just made it up. And when he told us it can hold 1,000 songs and fit into your pocket, those were the vows (a feature and its function) he committed to as descriptive of his new product declaration.

"I am your boss (or chief, or royal, or president, or god)." Made-up leadership declarations.

While declarations are clearly crafted in our imaginations, they still have meaning. Declarations come with commitments that must be adhered to or consequences will ensue. When our spouses don't live up to their vows, we divorce them. When products don't live up to their product data sheets, we return them. When our leaders don't prove worthy of our followership, we can shift our loyalties elsewhere (in democratic societies, anyway).

STORY TIME WITH GOLDY

For the eulogy, refer to line 52 where I first reference Doc as a renaissance man. As far as I know, neither I nor any of his friends had ever called him that. It was during the presentation planning process that I connected the dots between his personal and professional life that I decided to ***declare*** him as such. I just made it up using my authority as the eulogist.

Even though I declared it into existence, it doesn't mean that everyone immediately accepted my authority to do so. But I was committed to this declaration, so I continued in the eulogy to describe my reasoning. By the third or fourth time I uttered this speech act, I saw heads nodding in agreement.

Commit to some declarations about yourself, your product, service, idea, or organization in your presentation. Be prepared to articulate the vows for each declaration, either on the slide or in your voice over.

That concludes Part 1 of "**A ROAD** TO ACTION." I've created a mnemonic to help you remember the underlying distinctions. In this case:

- A=Assertions
- R=Requests (Part 2)
- O=Offers (Part 2)
- A=Assessments
- D=Declarations

As you walk through the rest of the design elements in the coming sections, you'll be liberally sprinkling assertions, assessments, and declarations throughout. Arriving at Step 6 in my process, you'll first learn more powerful distinctions of the last two Speech Acts—Requests and Offers—before crafting the final portion of your talk.

NEUROECONOMICS, YOU CAN BE MY WINGMAN ANYTIME

In the Introduction, I gave a very brief overview of neuroeconomics and my reasoning for using it as a framework for my process. Here I want to give you a more thorough understanding of the terminology because I'll be referring to the three components of the discourse throughout.

There's an old joke about how to quickly tell the difference between an introverted and extroverted engineer in a social setting. The introvert looks at their own shoes when conversing, while the extrovert looks at yours.

Delivering an oral presentation requires more than just subject area expertise. What the not-so-subtle joke above nudges us towards is a recognition that the more highly educated one is—scientist, engineer, mathematician, lawyer, doctor, accountant—the less likely they have studied the social sciences and understand what others have labeled emotional intelligence (EQ). The EQ skillset for persuading your listener to act can be as simple as coming up to you after your talk and asking for your business card or as uplifting as agreeing to sign a contract while writing you a check.

The declaration neuroeconomics brings together three distinct fields of study involved in understanding human decision-making under economic conditions.

Neuroscience: How the brain is organized and functions

Cognitive Psychology: Our use of language and memory

Behavioral Economics: Decision-making under risk and uncertainty

The recognition that these three disciplines belonged together emerged in the late 1990s with a kickstart from New York University Professor Paul Glimcher, who many consider the "father" of neuroeconomics, and the advent of functional magnetic resonance imaging *f*MRI.

You are probably very familiar with the imaging capabilities of a traditional MRI scanner. An *f*MRI uses a special feature to detect blood flow in the brain. Originally intended to help surgeons understand blood flow anomalies in patients that had a stroke or other forms of brain damage, neuroscientists realized with *f*MRI and other emerging brain scanning methods, they could figure out which parts of the brain are most active when processing inputs from our sensory systems.

For example, via *f*MRI studies, we now know there's a specific area of the brain called the *fusiform gyrus* that processes facial features, allowing us to recognize family and friends. An entirely different part of the brain recognizes non-facial shapes and colors. Having a rudimentary understanding of the brain's architecture and processing mechanisms is vital to the design of the text and graphics in our presentations. Similarly, the how and where of audio processing is essential to optimizing our selection, projection, and tonation of our spoken words.

Think of neuroeconomics as a military intelligence officer providing expertise to the strike planning team. Before we can go any further in our presentation mission planning, we need to understand the battlefield layout between our listeners two ears. Yes, it's a battlefield. Your speech is competing against all the internal and external distractions swimming around in our heads:

- I'm hungry, when are we going to eat?
- Did I leave the stove on when I left the house?
- Why is it so cold in here?
- I really shouldn't have sent that email as a reply all.
- I better bring a present home to my spouse to make up for my shitty behavior last night.
- I'm so tired right now, I wish I could just zzzzzzzzzzzz

Besides the purpose of your presentation, as we discussed in the beginning of this chapter, you must always manipulate your listener into focusing on what you have to say, literally at the expense of whatever else is going on inside their heads. This is why you need to understand the basics of neuroeconomics and its ability to manipulate your listeners so you can outcompete the other conversations inside their head.

WE'RE OBLIGATED TO MANIPULATE OUR LISTENERS

The best way to manipulate a man is to make him think he is manipulating you.

~ John Smith, 17th century explorer, author

Before you throw this book away and unfriend me from your social media, be patient as I explore with you an uncommon interpretation of manipulation.

The common dictionary definition is this: "Being able to control or influence a person or situation cleverly, unfairly, or unscrupulously."[8] That does sound rather diabolical, but let's understand the difference between ethical and unethical manipulation.

My claim in this book (and in my business education company) is that "ethical" behaviors in business are those that promote more satisfying customer relationships with resultant business growth. Good ethics are defined from your customer's perspective, or in the case of an oral presentation, your listener's viewpoint.

Let's imagine a form of manipulation that is fair from the customer's perspective. Think back to one or more of the following "firsts" you might have experienced as a child or young adult when learning a new sport or musical skill.

- The baseball coach adjusting how you swung the bat
- The tennis pro adjusting the grip on your racquet
- The golf pro adjusting your stance as you addressed the ball
- The gymnastics coach guiding you through that first back flip
- The equine instructor guiding your foot into the stirrup as you mounted the horse
- The swim instructor holding you the first time you floated on your back

---

8 https://www.merriam-webster.com/dictionary/manipulation

- The guitar teacher correctly placing your fingers on the fret to make a chord
- The violin teacher adjusting how you held the bow

In each of these examples the instructor is physically manipulating the student. And we (or our parents) were paying them to do so! In the case of the instructor-student relationship, the manipulation is quite explicit—"I'm paying you to help me with my golf swing."

Other times, the agreement to be manipulated is more implicit and subtle. For example, when we agree to allow our financial planner to manipulate our investments to increase the probability of higher returns. Or the university professor that manipulates our critical thinking skills so that we may interact with the world more successfully. Or the movie producer who manipulates our reality for a few hours for our own enjoyment. Or when a lawyer uses a persuasive argument to manipulate a client into accepting a plea deal because they know it has the best legal outcome for the client.

Whether it's physical, intellectual, or what I call ***ethical manipulation***—controlling or influencing our customers for the sake of ***taking care of <u>their</u> human and business concerns***—the customer has agreed to it and even expects it.

"Goldy, now that you've defined the positive side of the word, is there a way to recognize and avoid unethical manipulation?"

In my opinion, most advertising is unethical. Even before the formal invention of behavioral science, the Don Drapers of Madison Avenue (shout out to *Mad Men*) manipulated us to consumerism—driving the economy by buying consumer goods that most of us didn't need, shouldn't have bought, or couldn't afford.

My definition of unethical manipulation: using brain science more to your own benefit than your customers'.

With this awareness in mind, I encourage you to respect that your audience has given up their time and, perhaps, even paid a fee to hear your talk. They have become explicit customers of your ideas and expect to be manipulated, whether they say so or not. Your obligation then is to make it ethical. For their sake.

This alternative consideration of manipulation to mean something akin to "manage or utilize skillfully" is what makes the weapons school method so compelling. Every instructor is purposefully trained to ethically manipulate the listener for the listeners' benefit; to save their lives in combat. Throughout the rest of this book, as I expand your knowledge of neuroeconomics, you should be continuously thinking, "How can I use this to ethically manipulate my listener?"

RECAPPING SOME WORDS ABOUT WORDS

This concludes, for now, the list of essential words that is necessary to launch us into the remainder of our academic modules and presentation planning lessons.

Customer: *someone who buys your product, service, or idea*

Prospect: *a future customer*

Listener: *a customer or prospect who's listening to the description of your product, service, or idea*

Assertion: *a universally agreed upon factual definition that can be verified as true or false by an independent 3rd party*

Assessment: *an opinion that notices the past to predict the future; neither true nor false, rather grounded (by facts) or ungrounded (speculation)*

Neuroeconomics: *the study of the intersection of cognitive psychology, behavioral economics, and neuroscience*

Manipulation: *ethical or unethical behavioral alteration*

PART I

MISSION PLANNING

If you want me to give you a two-hour presentation,
I am ready today.
If you want only a five-minute speech,
it will take me two weeks to prepare.

~ Mark Twain

STEP 1: MAKE IT PURPOSEFUL

Before we start your classroom training, it's …

STORY TIME WITH GOLDY

I received the call asking me to give Dave's eulogy about two weeks prior to the event with instructions from his father, a retired judge, to limit my talk to five minutes. Thank you, ghost of Mark Twain. I had my mission. It was time to commence my presentation mission planning.

In the mid-80s, while both of us were stationed at Miramar, Dave and I were housemates. I had just returned from deployment, and he was a new member of Carrier Airwing FIFTEEN (CVW-15) staff. As an aerospace medicine officer (a.k.a. flight surgeon), "Doc" spent his days at the base medical clinic performing countless, mind-numbing flight physicals on some of the nation's healthiest warriors. Even when suffering from an ailment, pilots will lie about it to make sure they don't get grounded by the flight surgeon. He would reflect years later that this was his career low point.

One day, Doc came home incredibly animated. "Goldy, you'll never believe what I got to do today!"

I tried to look as excited as he was, "Tell me!"

"I got to resuscitate my first full cardiac arrest! I've been training for this since med school, but this is the first time ever on a real person! There was this sailor …"

He shared all the gruesome details. How it happened. Where he was when he got called. How long he had to perform it.

At some moment, I just had to ask, "So, what happened to the patient?"

"Oh, he died." (pause) "But I got to perform CPR! Isn't that great?!"

"Isn't that great?" was a Doc mantra. At the reception following the formal memorial service, there were many other anecdotes told of him that a friend capped off with, "Isn't this (or wasn't that) great?"

Like the time he and his squadron mate Robert "Lopes" Lopez were being chewed out by the airwing commander in a manner exactly reminiscent of the famous scene in the original *Top Gun* when CAG Stinger yells at Maverick and Goose for doing a high-speed flyby of the tower. Doc and Lopes had snuck away from their regularly scheduled programming to do something incredibly risky with a nearby Marine Corps detachment, and CAG was furious.

After Lopes and Doc left CAG's office, Doc turns to Lopes and said: "Wasn't that great?! He was yellin' at us just like in the movie!"

I share these two anecdotes not to disparage Doc's memory in any way. He was one of the most generous humanists I've ever known. But he was also a realist. He knew there was nothing he could've done to save that man's life. The sailor was an unhealthy, older leader with a thick medical record. So rather than wallow in sorrow, he relished the opportunity to apply his very expensively earned skills to the grim circumstances.

Armed with everything I knew about Doc including his joy of life, that I learned from eighteen years of friendship, I sat down to design the eulogy the way I do with even the most run-of-the-mill talks: What's my purpose and what's the due date?

PICK A CROWD, ANY CROWD

To help you think through your own presentation planning, I can easily imagine one of four possible scenarios that you are either facing today or likely to face soon. To assist you in your planning process, pick one and only one of the scenarios described in Table 1 and keep it front of mind as you design your own talk.

Table 1 — Presentation Scenarios

Scenario	Name	Situation
1	Inform the Industry	You have volunteered (or been "voluntold") to give an informative presentation at an industry event (tradeshow, conference, technical symposium) highlighting an idea, project, accomplishment, your company's new product or service, etc.
2	Pitch the Prospect	A prospective customer (prospect in sales terminology) is scheduled to hear about you or your organization's portfolio of existing products and/or ideas for a new product or service. Think Japan's *Money Tigers* or the US franchise version *Shark Tank,* minus the cat fights, of course.
3	Compel the Customer	In response to a solicitation–a request for proposal (RFP), request for quote (RFQ), tender, or email scope change–you must give an oral presentation that compels the customer to buy or invest in your (or your company's) product or service.
4	Persuade the PM	You are assigned to a team executing a customer's program that requires delivering oral presentations at specific intervals or milestones (monthly status reports, design reviews, test results) to the customer's Program Manager (PM).

Before writing even one word, or designing your first slide, take as much time as you need to understand the talk's purpose. I suggest starting with the following question:

"What outcome do I want to produce at the end of my talk?"

To answer this, you will need to know where in the Customer Relationship Cycle (a.k.a. Sales Cycle) you are currently located.

GO AHEAD, SELL ME THIS PEN

We all have something of value to exchange to live our lives. Everyone lives by selling something.

~ Robert Louis Stevenson

Regardless of which scenario you're faced with, I want you to become comfortable with the interpretation that each one is, at its core, a sales conversation echoing Robert Louis Stevenson's claim that we're all in the business of selling. Engineers sell their design ideas to technical leads. Managers sell their competence to business owners. Lawyers sell arguments to judges and juries. Parents sell their children on eating their vegetables. Selling is part of the human condition. In its purest sense, giving an oral presentation is selling something to your listener(s), regardless if it's an audience of 1 or 1,001.

It is beyond the scope of this book to go through a detailed discussion about selling and customer relationships. But you do need to have a sense of it.

A web search of the term "sales cycle" or "customer relationship cycle" reveals a variety of process maps with between five and ten stages. The version I use in my workshop has seven stages (Figure 1). I trust the labels at each stage, starting at the top of the cycle, are self-explanatory regarding the associated activity.

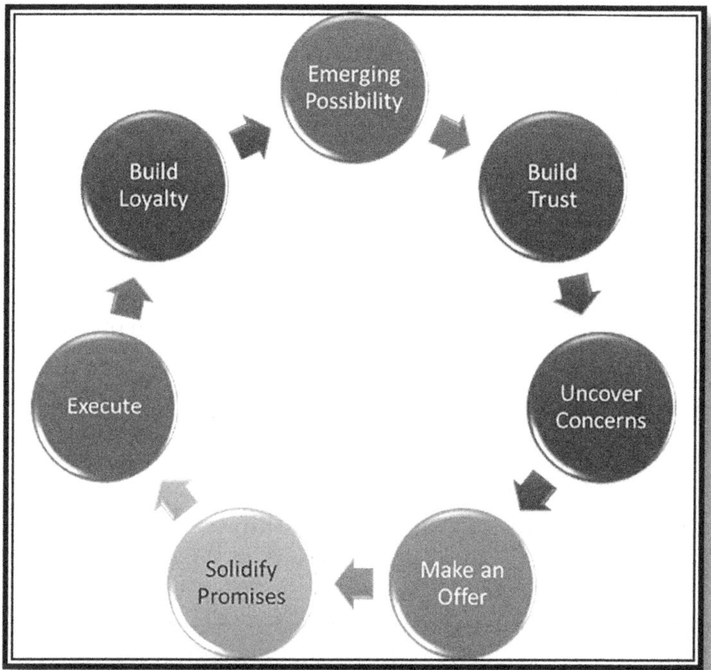

FIGURE 1 — CUSTOMER RELATIONSHIP CYCLE

Whether you accept my seven-stage process or are more familiar with your own company's process, ignore the differences for a moment and focus on the common features found in all sales cycles. For example, its circular versus linear nature. This implies that the shortest path to a new sale is to build on the success of the prior sale.

This is as true in delivering oral presentations as it is in product sales. I recently gave an educational webinar to a proposal writing organization's online conference. The positive feedback from the attendees very quickly opened an opportunity for me to speak in person at their upcoming annual live event in Amsterdam. In both cases, I'm selling my value as a corporate consultant in the professional proposal writing community.

Notice that each stage builds upon the last. As you move your way around the circle from the top, you have a more informed, closer relationship with your customer (customer being defined most generically as your listener). As you advance, your presentation becomes more intimate, thoughtful, and customized.

Finally, imagine a highly consequential presentation, such as persuading the board of directors of a large multinational conglomerate to merge with another company. In this example, you will most likely have to repeat the cycle multiple times as you first brief the company's mergers and acquisitions director followed by the CEO, and, when all the kinks are ironed out, you will finally present the idea to the full board.

With each turn around the cycle, the presentation will require modifications to address the specific concerns of the listener. The Mergers and Acquisitions Director may want to focus on the financial and process details while the CEO dives deeper into the overall corporate strategy, with the board needing to understand how the merger might require regulatory approval.

In Figure 2, I have overlaid the four possible oral presentation scenarios listed earlier on top of the customer relationship cycle. In Table 2, I've listed some of the possible purposes associated with each stage.

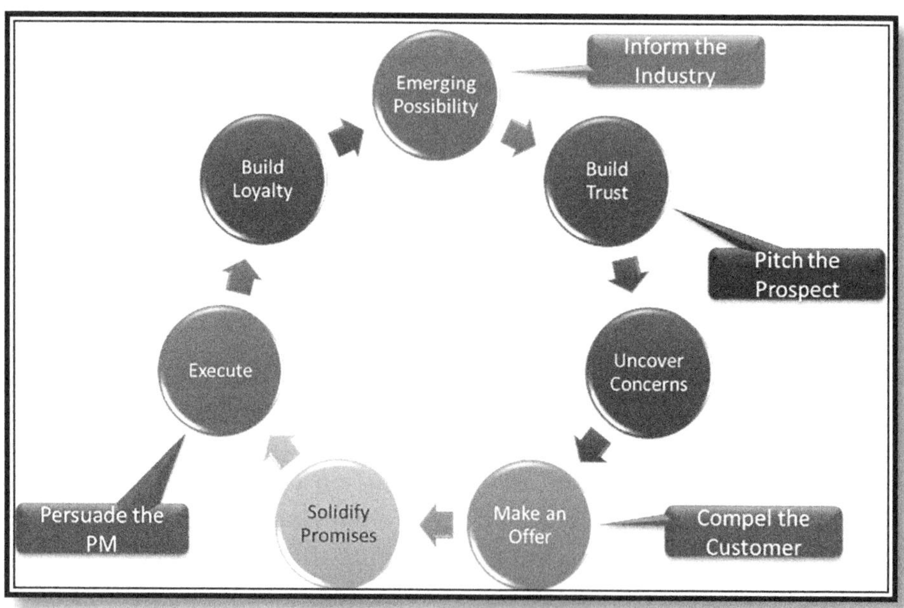

FIGURE 2 — ORAL PRESENTATION CYCLE WITH SCENARIOS

Table 2 — Defining Your Presentation's Purpose

Presentation Type	Possible Purpose(s)
Inform the Industry	To attract members of the audience to join your team, apply for a job at your company, anticipate the launch of your new product...
Pitch the Prospect	To begin establishing an assessment of trustworthiness such that the prospect recognizes that you care for their concerns. To create a future opportunity to invent something new together.
Compel the Customer	To offer help that the customer recognizes is essential to their continued survival. To request your customer sign a contract, give a down payment, agree to schedule a meeting with the decision maker.
Persuade the PM	To solidify your trustworthiness such that the PM chooses to continue the project and/or give you additional assignments (and funds) to complete. Persuade the PM to agree with your recommendations.

For Doc's eulogy, I was clear that this was an "Inform the Industry" type. I was there to sell a more complete, uplifting memory of someone we all loved dearly. Like the story about Doc performing CPR for the first time, I wanted the assembled masses to go away from the eulogy with an inner voice that, like Doc's might have said: "Oh yeah, he died … but I got to go to an incredible memorial service at Arlington National Cemetery. Isn't that great?!"

Bottom line: You have spent considerable time preparing your talk. Your audience is sacrificing their "lost opportunity" time to listen to your talk when there's an almost infinite number of alternatives … on TikTok alone! Don't disrespect the value of your time or theirs by straying from purpose(s).

MAKE IT PURPOSEFUL CHECKLIST

As I describe in Part 3—The Weapons School Way, there's a daily rhythm to the training stages at TOPGUN and its sibling weapons schools as shown in Table 3:

TABLE 3 — DAILY WEAPONS SCHOOL TRAINING REGIMEN

Stage	Duration	Description
Classroom Academics	1 – 2 hours	Deep dive into a particular aircraft system, weapon or combat flying technique.
Mission Planning	1 – 2 hours	Students plan a training flight (or simulator) whose objectives are to test the student's comprehension and application of the classroom module.
Simulator or Training Flight	1 – 1.5 hours	Students fly a simulated combat mission in a high-fidelity simulator or in their jets on a training range against other aircraft that are configured to replicate various adversaries.

In Part 3b, titled Here a Check, There a Check, I describe how all of aviation, military or civilian, rely on checklists to start, taxi, takeoff, fly, land, and shutdown their aircraft. I even give an example of an actual checklist from the A-6 Intruder I used to fly during my second weapons school instructor tour. I encourage you to at least skim that section so that the rest of this module will make more sense to you.

In any case, here's your checklist for the equivalent of the very first checklist in every aircraft's operating manual—the "Walkaround Inspection."

MAKE IT PURPOSEFUL

1. Audience scenario...SELECT
    a. Inform the Industry
    b. Pitch the Prospect
    c. Compel the Customer
    d. Persuade the PM

NOTE

It's important to have one and only one of these scenarios in mind at a time. Changing the scenario will almost always require substantial revisions to an existing presentation design.

2. Sales cycle stages and purposes..REVIEW
3. Preliminary PURPOSE ....SELECT

NOTE

Do not proceed any further until you have made this preliminary selection. Unlike the Scenario selection, you will have an opportunity to adjust prior to takeoff (e.g.,, rehearsal stage).

STEP 2: MAKE IT PERSONAL

We take for granted we know the whole story. We judge a book by its cover and read what we want between selected lines.

- Axl Rose

Our goal with oral presentations is, as the saying goes, to win their hearts and minds and gain their emotional and intellectual agreement with our position. To achieve this, we need to understand how to ethically manipulate their decision-making process. This is where neuroeconomics comes into play. In this chapter, we will focus our attention on the neuroscience component—how our brains are organized and function.

WARNING: CONTROVERSY AHEAD

There's general agreement in the neuroscience community that there's no such thing as free will. Every feeling, thought, and action can be understood at the level of neurons by analyzing the biological, historical, and social experiences of a specific human. Even if you are unwilling to accept this theory of human behavior, I claim that you can still have more success in the design and delivery of your talk if you act as if it's true.

Stanford University's Robert Sapolsky explains human decision-making through the lens of chemical signaling that happens in the brain seconds, hours, generations, and millions of years before.[9] To compel our listeners to a "yes," we need to know how their brain compares and calculates the available sensory input signals—visual, aural, olfactory, tactile, and tasteful. As the highly acclaimed *Mad Men* television series that lifted the skirt, both figuratively and literally, on 20th century marketing as a discipline demonstrated, the truth is that the marketing and advertising industry has been manipulating us for decades. We're constantly being manipulated,

---

9 Robert Sapolsky, *Behave: The biology of humans at our best and worst* (Penguin, 2017).

even more so now with the advent of social media algorithms. By exposing how this works to enhance your presentations, as a positive side effect, you will also learn to become a more prudent consumer yourself.

Let's begin this manipulative journey by understanding how our brains evolved.

A BRIEF HISTORY OF HOMINID TIME

I accept the assertion that we live on the "*3rd Rock from The Sun*" (shoutout to the underrated NBC show) which congealed from stardust about 4.5 billion years ago. The rest of our evolutionary history follows from the same scientific dating methods discerned by researchers starting with the appearance of simple life forms about 500 million years after the earth formed. Complex, multicellular life appeared some 2 billion years later still and then came the good stuff.

Long before the 1960s, the real sexual revolution occurred about 2 billion years ago when male and female eukaryotes skipped the vodka, cranberry juice, orange juice, and peach schnapps, and went straight to having actual sex on the beach. Without any venture capital funding, life started experimenting with its own form of recombinant DNA for the next 1.5 billion years and, *Voilà*! the Cambrian Explosion produced a flood of land animals—reptiles, dinosaurs, and legacy automotive manufacturers. Approximately 200 million years ago the first mammals appeared. Then came the global financial crisis of 1929 A.D., I mean, asteroid crash of 66 million B.C., which turned out the lights in the Yucatan Peninsula followed by a months-long, worldwide blackout, spoiling even the chilled shrimp in the underwater freezers at the earth's poles.

Like New York City subway rodents, ocean bottom-feeders feasted on a veritable smorgasbord as starving sea life higher up in the water column rained down for hundreds of years. Like Tom Brady's never-ending American football career, life hung on long enough to survive and thrive until our hominid ancestors emerged approximately 6 million years ago. This was a crucial moment in our pre-human history because this is where we started developing culture. Millions of years before the rise of WFH (work from home) and the fall of the daily commute, the underpinnings of what Migliano and Vinicius refer to as "social egalitarianism, sexual and social division of labor, extensive coresidence and cooperation with unrelated individuals … engendered a multilevel social structure".[10] [Yes, that was as hard to write as it was to read.]

In other words, as our primate ancestors emerged from the mammalian evolutionary soup, we started working together in larger and larger groups. Instead of a pride of lions, a herd of elephants, or a troop of chimps with at most two dozen members all related to each other as siblings or cousins, tribes of ancient humans found strength in numbers—up to 150 hunter-gatherers holding annual shareholder meetings. Men and women were often exchanged between these pre-historic corporate entities to keep their respective gene pools from needing chlorine.

No matter how culturally sophisticated we think we are we're still animals inside and it takes a tremendous expenditure of cognitive force to overcome our predilections for judgmental behavior as the following sections will illustrate.

Omne trium perfectum – WHAT COMES IN THREES IS PERFECT

Looking at the evolutionary path I just described, physician and neuroscientist Paul MacLean proposed a Triune Brain Model[11] (a.k.a. "three brain theory") to describe, in simple terms, the evolution of the human brain. In MacLean's theory, the brain evolved in three stages starting with the most primitive, "reptilian" core (a.k.a. croc brain or brain stem) that controls most of our instinctual and autonomic functions. A crocodile has no ethics or social skills. It knows three things—aggression, eating, and reproducing. I colloquially refer to these core capabilities as the 3 Fs—feeding, fighting, and fornicating—and they're still extant deep down in our skulls. As mammals appeared in our evolutionary tree, the limbic system (a.k.a. midbrain) became the seat of socialization functions that allows us mammals to survive and thrive in mutually supportive social groups (e.g., a cackle of hyenas, a flock of sheep, a herd of elephants, bowling leagues, and LinkedIn). Finally, as hominids emerged some three

10 Andrea Bamber Migliano and Lucio Vinicius, "The origins of human cumulative culture: from the foraging niche to collective intelligence" in *Philosophical Transactions of the Royal Society B*, 377 (1843), 20200317.

11 Paul MacLean, *The Triune Brain in Evolution: Role in paleocerebral functions* (Springer Science & Business Media, 1990).

million years ago, the neocortex evolved, leading to the higher reasoning we (sometimes) observe in our fellow humans. Table 4 below summarizes the key features and functions as theorized by MacLean.

Table 4 — MacLean's Triune Brain

Layer	Key Features	Functions
Brain Stem (Croc Brain)	Automatic systems	Keep the body in homeostasis – body hydrated, blood oxygenated, appetite satiated, thermally regulated – and procreating.
Limbic	Emotional responses	Social sensing (love, hate, fear, reward, status).
Neocortex	Reasoning and mood	Do the difficult but right thing. Make assessments of your situation – confidence, resignation, ambition, despair.

Neuroscientists now know that the brain, like Europe's rail system, is highly interconnected, with neurons projecting their signals between, through, and around the three regions that MacLean postulated. For that reason, purists argue against MacLean's overly simplistic description. However, for the purpose of designing an oral presentation, it serves us well to apply our TTPs to specifically target the three evolutionary layers—croc, limbic, neocortex.

A TALE OF TWO SYSTEMS – SYSTEM 1

While MacLean described the structure of the brain, psychologists Daniel Kahneman and Amos Tversky focused instead on its functional capability, specifically regarding decision-making. Their work together, excellently chronicled in Michael Lewis' *The Undoing Project*, ultimately led to Kahneman's 2002 award of the Nobel Memorial Prize in Economic Sciences, a first for a psychologist.[12] Instead of a three-layered model,

12 Kahneman and others believe that Tversky would have also been so honored but for his untimely death a few years prior which, by arcane rules, permits only the living to receive the

Kahneman proposed a theory of two interconnected "agents". System 1 is our highly intuitive, instinctual, automatic, fast, parallel processor and System 2 is our rational, logical, slow, indecisive, serial processor.[13] The terms System 1 and System 2 are widely used in both academic literature and consumer writing but often to indicate a competitive nature between them. Or that they operate independently of each other. Nothing could be further from the truth.

While the attributes listed in Table 5 are categorized by their respective system, the two are always working side-by-side in a cooperative attempt to increase the probability of our survival. In high stress situations where immediate action is required, we generally follow System 1's guidance whereas System 2 has greater influence in more deliberative settings.

Table 5 - Two Cerebral Systems Protect One Physical Body

System 1	System 2
Unconscious	Conscious effort
Fast, parallel processing	Slow, serial processing
Associative	Logical
Decisive	Indecisive
Automatic Pilot	Lazy

Now that we know a bit about both the structure and the function of our listener's brain, let's explore how they impact our presentation mission planning, starting with one of our most basic survival instincts—recognizing danger.

DAMN YANKEES

♪[Insert Pink Floyd musical accompaniment here.]♪

Us (us, us, us, us) and them (them, them, them, them)/
And after all we're only ordinary men

~ **Lyrics by Roger Waters,** Pink Floyd

award.

13 Daniel Kahneman, *Thinking, Fast and Slow* (Macmillan, 2011).

♪[Insert Sesame Street musical accompaniment here.]♪

One of these things is not like the other/
One of these things doesn't belong/
Can you tell which thing is not like the other/
By the time I finish my song/

~ **Adapted from the Sesame Street,**
song written by Joe Rapaso and Jon Stone

Humans are preprogrammed to immediately recognize and react to situations we haven't experienced before.

One of our brain's most important automatic functions is pattern matching. As Figure 3 shows, when receiving sensory inputs (Step 1), the brain assembles the inputs into a pattern (Step 2) and then tries to match the pattern (Step 3) with something it has previously seen (or heard, smelled, felt, or tasted). It doesn't have to be an exact match. If it's close, the brain will fill in missing pieces to make it match. Hence, the reason optical illusions work so well and why you can still make out the voice of your own child crying in a room full of other "rugrats."

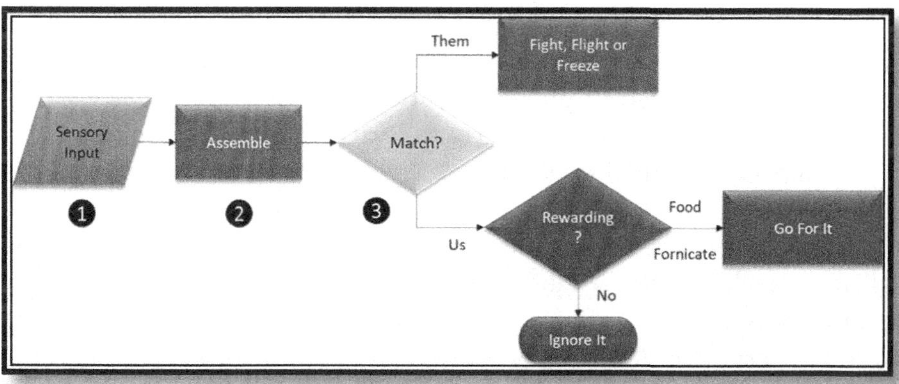

FIGURE 3 - OUR BRAIN THE MATCHMAKER

And this is where it gets interesting and politically incorrect. The matching algorithm is basically an "Us" versus "Them" System 1 decision. If the match is something that we recognize as a threat or don't recognize at all, then our "Them" fear response unconsciously kicks in and activates the flight, fight, or freeze mechanism.

If the match is recognizable as a non-threatening "Us," it tries to recall whether it's useful—something that helps it survive or something that helps its genes survive. Remember, our croc brain only knows the 3 F's (fight, food, fornicate). Since we're not on the "fight" path in the algorithm, and if it's neither food nor fornicate, then we ignore it and move on to the next sensory input.

For an interesting viewpoint, check out Jaclyn Kain's article about how our brains interpret food and sex with the same reward system.[14]

Breakfast in bed anyone?

This Us versus Them response has some morally troublesome but instinctually normal consequences as reported by researchers like Stanford University's Robert Sapolsky. Our System 1 fear and aggression reaction is triggered in less than one tenth of a second when spotting another race face. It takes hundreds of milliseconds more for our more rational System 2 to overcome this implicit bias. As told by Sapolsky,

> "... stick your average person in a brain scanner and show him a picture of someone of another race for only a tenth of a second. This is too fast for him to be aware of what he saw. But thanks to [an] anatomical shortcut, the amygdala knows . . . and activates. In contrast, show the picture for a longer time. Again the amygdala activates, but then the cognitive dlPFC [dorsolateral prefrontal cortex] does as well, inhibiting the amygdala—the effort to control what is for most people an unpalatable initial response.[15]

Funnily enough, this subconscious bias also shows up for strong social alliances such as when a rabid New York Yankees *Us* (count me in that camp) spots a *Them* wearing a Boston Red Sox cap. Or whenever a Navy TOPGUN spots an Air Farce, oops, Air Force pilot singing "Who's got that loving feeling" to a Charlie in one of *our* officer's clubs.

The Us versus Them algorithm is incredibly strong and deeply instinctual. Again, watch a David Attenborough BBC special and notice how pack species of all types, from meerkats to macaques and lions to

---

14 https://spoonuniversity.com/lifestyle/food-and-sex-are-the-same-to-your-brain

15 Robert Sapolsky, Behave: The Biology of Humans at Our Best and Worst (Penguin, 2017), 39.

lemurs, immediately recognize when members of their own species but from a different tribe of Thems have invaded their territory. Once spotted or smelled, the automatic threat response leads to alarm bells among group members.

Indigenous peoples have, for centuries, used face and body paint, piercings, and head dresses, to distinguish themselves from competing tribes. In more modern times, specific gang-related tattoos explicitly warn Thems to be wary.

System 2 reasoning alone is rarely enough to combat these System 1 biological prejudices. As many have said: You cannot reason someone out of a belief that they weren't reasoned into.

Why does this matter to oral presentations? As a presenter, the audience will naturally be pre-disposed to view you as a Them as soon as you step to the front of the room. Your goal then is to override this System 1 response and quickly compel their System 2 into a more receptive Us reaction. This was well-illustrated in both *Top Gun* movies. Wearing either a uniform or a flight suit in front of the class immediately informs the audience that the instructor was an Us. Notice in the original movie when Kelly McGillis' "Charlie" is in front of the class discussing fighter tactics, the body language of the students in the room emitted skepticism and distrust—an Us response to a non-military academician.

Your goal as a presenter is to find as many connections as you can to your listener to avoid Them and produce an Us interpretation. I hardly ever say this publicly but thank the Internet for social media. Before I ever talk to a prospect for the first time, I always check their online profiles or talk with one of their colleagues / assistants first so I can find an intersection. As a Jewish, white, male, Jersey Boy, Northwestern University-educated computer scientist, retired naval officer, US FAA commercial pilot with an instrument rating, living in Spain, speaking Spanish, having visited more than 40 countries, with the ability to say please and thank you in 25 languages, I cannot remember a time when I couldn't find at least one Us attribute to ethically exploit.

STORY TIME WITH GOLDY

I was helping a client on a competitive bid for a US government project. In profiling the government's PM, we discovered that he and my client's PM had worked for the same government agency at different times in their career. *Voila*! On the client PM's resume, which was included as part of the proposal submission, we made sure to include logos for all the organizations where he worked. This ensured that the government PM's eye would immediately recognize the logo even if he skimmed over the words, thus triggering an Us response.

Which brings me to the next module where I provide TTPs for ethically profiling your listener to help you discover their Us connections.

I SPIE WITH MY LITTLE EYE

It is more important to know what sort of person has a disease than to know what sort of disease a person has.

~ Hippocrates

WARNING: MORE CONTROVERSY AHEAD

There is an entire body of work in adult learning theory that explores cultural diversity in the classroom[16, 17, 18, 19]. The consensus opinion of the research concludes that who we are and where we came from—e.g.,, our gender identity, race, native language, nationality, religion—matters greatly to how well we can learn and, most importantly, how we operate in learning teams. Ignoring these differences in the classroom by treating everyone identically produces a feeling of invisibility, of delegitimizing the student's social and historical background. In other words, the best teachers are those that recognize and embrace our differences and bring them to the fore in the classroom.

Unfortunately, in the workplace, I have both observed and personally experienced the opposite. In a well-meaning attempt to avoid even the slightest "micro-aggression" in conversation, we are told to shun questions about someone's identity if we notice that they dress, talk, or look differently than we do.

As an educator, I don't subscribe to the philosophy of everyone being equal. We are not! The world is made up of billions of unique individuals. I don't want to be treated like some blended average.

I am a male, Jewish, American, Jerseyite, computer engineer, Naval officer, pilot, once widowed, currently married, father of two adult girls and one preteen boy, grandfather of three, native English speaking, DELE A2-level Spanish speaking, educator, skills trainer, coach, salesman, martial artist, piano-playing, chocolate-addicted, cigar-smoking, public speaker. Pick any one or more of those attributes to connect with me on an Us level.

No matter how much we're told "Don't judge a book by its cover," that advice conflicts with millions of years of primate evolution. University of Chicago Booth School of Business Professor of Psychology Alexander Todorov's detailed research on our facial recognition processes highlights

---

16 McIntosh, P. *White privilege: Unpacking the invisible knapsack.* 1990.

17 Anne Campbell, "Cultural identity as a social construct" in *Intercultural Education, 11*(1), 2000, 31-39.

18 Sharan B. Merriam and Mazaneh Mohamad, "How cultural values shape learning in older adulthood: The case of Malaysia" in *Qualitative research in practice: Examples for discussion and analysis,* 2002, 40-57.

19 Eugena K. Griffin, "Psychosocial techniques used in the classroom to captivate non-traditional community college students" in *Community College Journal of Research and Practice,* 44(5), 2020, 329-346.

the many ways we subconsciously divide our species into Us and Them based solely on how somebody looks.[20] There's more to it than just fear. We also pre-judge whether their smiles are genuine or forced and whether they're trustworthy or not.

To ignore our face value attributes goes against both our biology and psychology. Therefore, I created this learning module to help you ethically profile your listener to understand why they might consider you a Them and how to shift their System 1 response towards an Us. Regardless of your feelings on profiling, I ask you to consider the ability to form more intimate relationships with your listeners by leaning into it instead of brushing it under the rug. In other words, be fully present to the biological, historical, and social facts that have individually shaped all seven plus billion of us.

There are four categories of attributes to consider when profiling your listener: their Sex, Posture, Identity, and Epoch (SPIE is the mnemonic).

S FOR SEX

I could be politically correct and say that the sex of either the speaker or the listener is not important, but that simply isn't true. All the research points to two important aspects of biological sex in the context of oral presentations. First, our brains are sexually dimorphic—the scientific term for the fact that the brains of men and women are structurally different. Neuropsychiatrist Louann Brizendine reports on a very specific yet profound example of such dimorphic development that occurs at the tail end of the second month of fetal development when the brain goes through its first transformation programmed by sex hormones.

> A huge testosterone surge beginning in the eighth week will turn this unisex brain male by killing off some cells in the communication centers and growing more cells in the sex and aggression centers. If the testosterone surge doesn't happen, the female brain continues to grow unperturbed. The fetal girl's brain cells sprout more connections in the communication centers and areas that process emotion. How does this fetal fork in the road affect us? For one thing, because of her larger communication center, this girl will grow up to be more talkative than her brother. In most social contexts, she will use many

20 Alexander Todorov, *Face Value* (Princeton University Press, 2017).

> more forms of communication than he will. For another, it defines our innate biological destiny, coloring the lens through which each of us views and engages the world.[21]

In addition to enhanced communication skills, girls grow up with brain circuits better suited "for gathering meaning from faces and tone of voice".[22] In practical terms, we can expect female members of the audience to be more aware of the speakers' body language and speech patterns while the men focus more on the content.

The second important aspect of a listener's sex is to recognize how men and women behave differently when in the presence of the opposite sex—more accurately, mostly just men behave differently. Surprise, surprise. From Sapolsky:

> Another rapid social-context effect shows men in some of their lamest moments. Specifically, when women are present, or when men are prompted to think about women, they become more risk-taking, show steeper temporal discounting in economic decisions, and spend more on luxury items (but not on mundane expenses). Moreover, the allure of the opposite sex makes men more aggressive—for example, more likely in a competitive game to punish the opposing guy with loud blasts of noise. Crucially, this is not inevitable—in circumstances where status is achieved through prosocial routes, the presence of women makes men more prosocial. As summarized in the title of one paper demonstrating this, this seems a case of 'Male generosity as a mating signal'."[23]

I hope you picked up on my selection of sex and not gender or gender identity in my terminology. Two reasons. One flippant—I couldn't craft a catchy mnemonic with the letter 'g'.

The second reason is more thoughtful. In some, if not many, families around the world, there was, and may still be, a certain conditioning of how to "properly" raise each gender. Boys were (perhaps still are) raised

---

21 Louann Brizendine, *The Female Brain.* (Harmony/Rodale, 2007), 36.

22 Brizendine, *The Female Brain,* 38.

23 Sapolsky, *Behave,* 95.

surrounded by blue things and are given high-energy toys to play with (e.g., cars, trains, dump trucks), while girls were (perhaps still are) offered pink and given dolls and dress up clothes. I'm not saying I agree with this nor am I saying this is a universal construct. I only point this out because gender distinctions for humans are complex and emotionally charged topics within communities, religions, and political discourse. But in a surprising study from the 1950s by Robert Goy, Sapolsky reports:

> Old World primates are highly dimorphic; males are more aggressive, and females spend more time at affiliative behaviors (e.g., social grooming, interacting with infants). How's this for a sex difference: in one study, adult male rhesus monkeys were far more interested in playing with "masculine" human toys (e.g., wheeled toys) than "feminine" ones (stuffed animals), while females had a slight preference for feminine.[24]

This view of sex differences influencing play behavior preference has been echoed and even more fully described by Joyce Benenson of Harvard's Human Evolutionary Biology lab in her seminal book *Warriors and Worriers: The Survival of the Sexes*.[25]

In his widely popular and thought-provoking treatise *Sapiens*, historian Yuval Harari spends a great deal of time walking us through the historical roots of male domination across most societies, both ancient and modern. It is the rare exception where women are in charge. Harari exhaustively examined all the classic arguments why men have remained in charge, even in the face of immense social pressure today to legalize same sex marriage worldwide and legislate gender pay equality. He frustratedly ended his exploration thusly:

> These dramatic changes are precisely what makes the history of gender so bewildering. If, as is being demonstrated today so clearly, the patriarchal system has been based on unfounded myths rather than on biological facts, what accounts for the universality and stability of this system?[26]

---

24 Sapolsky, *Behave,* 213.

25 Joyce F. Benenson, *Warriors and Worriers: The survival of the sexes.* (Oxford University Press, 2014).

26 Yuval Noah Harari, *Sapiens (A Brief History)* (Harper, 2015) 160.

Once again, the nature versus nurture debate provides conflicting evidence. The takeaway for you as a presenter is to not ignore our sex differences but rather, in an ethically manipulative way, lean into the biological influences that specific male and female hormones have on our behavior and communication.

The primary biological differences between men and women result from varying levels of two key hormones: testosterone and estrogen. You likely know that both hormones circulate throughout the bodies of both sexes not just during adolescence but throughout life. The main difference is their relative levels. The average male has higher levels of testosterone while the average female has higher levels of estrogen. But there are also women with naturally high levels of testosterone and men with naturally high levels of estrogen.

Why does this matter to a presenter?

Let me offer you some scenarios that impact the design of your presentation.

- Testosterone + Oxytocin (the love hormone): In the presence of women, men tend to be more generous due to testosterone plus oxytocin.
- Testosterone + Dopamine (the reward hormone): Male investment managers take far more financial risks than women.
- Higher Testosterone: Higher aggression, math scores, assertiveness, ADHD, autism.
- Higher Estrogen: Women are more prone to anorexia, depression, anxiety.[27, 28, 29]

Let me wrap up this section with an alibi. As I mentioned already, not only did I avoid using the word gender but also sexual identity, sexual preference, gender identity, and all relevant pronouns. These are hot topics

27 M.B. Tamburrino and R.A. McGinnis "Anorexia nervosa. A review" in *Panminerva medica,* 44(4), 2022, 301-311.

28 Christine Kuehner, "Why is depression more common among women than among men?" in *The Lancet Psychiatry,* 4(2), 2017, 146-158.

29 Osvaldo Almeida, et al., "Anxiety, depression, and comorbid anxiety and depression: risk factors and outcome over two years" in *International Psychogeriatrics,* 24(10), 2012, 1622-1632.

for social scientists, the scope of which goes well beyond the purpose of the book. In the absence of our ability to scan our listener's brain or analyze their DNA to determine their brain's sex orientation, I leave the difficult job to the presenter to do their best in applying this new knowledge of biological sex.

Design your presentations to be "gender***ful***" versus gender neutral.

P FOR POSTURE

The Superman pose. Everyone knows it. Standing tall, fists on hips, elbows out, chest out, shoulders back. A surefire power posture. Compare that to the scene from the original *Top Gun* when Maverick tells his "…there I was upside down with the MiG" story. There are twelve aircrew in the classroom, all but one sitting back, slouched into their chairs, many with arms folded in a "I can't believe I have to sit here and listen to his bullshit" mood.

Returning to non-fictional, natural examples, David Attenborough and his crew have filmed amazing examples of power postures. From antelopes tipping their antlers to monkeys displaying their molars, wild animals rely on body language to both incite and sooth the wild beast. Here are some useful postural TTPs from the US National Park Service to execute during a surprise bear encounter.[30]

- "Make yourselves look as large as possible…"
- "Brown/Grizzly Bears: … leave your pack on and PLAY DEAD. Lay flat on your stomach with your hands clasped behind your neck."

Good advice in the wild. Not so good if you insult Will Smith's wife at an Academy Award ceremony.

30 https://www.nps.gov/subjects/bears/safety.htm

Whenever we walk into a room full of people, we have a System 1 response to posture. We subconsciously notice who's approachable and who isn't—who the alphas are in the room. Our ability to quickly discern a threatening versus submissive posture in the wild was a survival skill that has become useful in the urban jungle. Former Federal Bureau of Investigation (FBI) interrogator Joe Navarro, in his 2008 masterpiece *What Every Body is Saying* book and online videos explain how to more powerfully notice, observe, and assess body language as an essential business skill.[31]

You must hone your skills in displaying a presenter's posture (more on this in a later section) and reading the body language of your audience especially when delivering a high consequence pitch, specifically in front of small groups with a decision maker present. And, as we saw in the previous section, women are more attuned to reading such signals, so you men must train harder to master this skill.

I'm sure you've noticed this in your own life. Corporate leaders and managers tend to be more upright both when standing and sitting. Introverts tend to slouch when sitting and roll their shoulders forward when standing. Notice how that posture can also be affected by mood. In *Top Gun: Maverick*, Rooster's anxious mood shows up in the training scene as he leans forward, changing his posture in his chair, to see if Maverick can perform the mission in less than the stated timing challenge.

STORY TIME WITH GOLDY

In my final tour in the Navy, pre-9/11, I was leading a "feasibility study" to explore how to integrate unmanned surveillance aircraft more tactically into military operations. At the time, unmanned aircraft were considered to be solely for reconnaissance when missions were planned and executed by the intelligence forces. At the Naval Strike and Air Warfare Center (NSAWC), we had a theory that closer, more integrated, real-time coordination during strike and other offensive missions would increase mission success while reducing risks for manned aircraft crews.

31 Joe Navarro, and Marvin Karlins. *What Every Body is Saying An Ex-FBI Agent's Guide to Speed-Reading People* (William Morrow, 2008).

This was a Scenario 2, Pitch the Prospect, situation for me and my team of contractors. We had been given a $640,000 budget to put together a test and evaluation plan for the next three years that would require approximately $25 million of military funds to execute—a rounding error compared to the entire military budget but a huge investment to bring such a highly visible project to NAS Fallon. The $25 million pot of gold would only be granted to the best idea from all the services, so our project was competing against the Air Force and Army proposal (we had already won the internal Navy competition).

Off I went to military bases around the world, from Camp Humphreys, Korea, to Ramstein in Germany, presenting to stakeholders looking for feedback and endorsements. At a minimum, we always traveled as a pair, one to present, one to sit in the back of the room, take notes, and, most importantly, watch the body language of the audience. You can tell a lot about a person's social power—the sway they hold with their colleagues—just by observing where and how they sit. We could also largely predict their receptiveness to our concept by giving more credence to their body language than their words alone.

Become an observer of Posture. Practice it both in social and professional settings.

I FOR IDENTITY

When I first started driving motorcycles as a 20-something, I noticed an unusual behavior from other riders. As they passed me, they would hold out their hand with just one or two extended fingers at a low angle towards the pavement, about hip height. Called the "Biker Wave," it's a gesture that says, "Hey, good to see another rebel out on the road today." This is the way we identified ourselves as bikers. Not to be confused with cyclists, whom

I'd never wave to because they wear colorful shirts, padded pants, no socks, and I don't want to encourage such fashionistas. I'll stick with my leathers.

Uh, sorry, that was my testosterone talking again.

In the animal kingdom, prey animals use coloration as a survival mechanism to warn predators to take notice before attacking, something scientists call aposematism (think coral snake, poison arrow frog, and skunk).

We humans do it too, often going much further with our signaling. We use tattoos to claim allegiance to our career, loved ones, a favorite sports club, and even commercial products. It goes well beyond being inked. At its core, there's little difference between showing your MS-13 tattoo on the streets of Los Angeles, strutting your stuff on the Champs-Élysées with a Gucci handbag over your bent arm, wearing *payos* (sidecurls) and a *shtreimel* (fur hat) in Borough Park, Brooklyn, or proudly displaying a Manchester United T-shirt while walking to the big match with rival Liverpool. These are all survival signals letting others know that you want to be identified as part of a distinct gang, social class, religion, fan club, or whatever. We announce our identity by all our external markings, whether removable or not.

Arizona State University's Professor Emeritus of Psychology Robert Cialdini reports on some remarkable findings regarding how we grant power to certain people and not others based solely on their attire. Reporting on a study by Lefkowitz, Blake, and Mouton published in 1955, Cialdini summarized the study as follows:

> Research conducted in Texas, for instance, arranged for a thirty-one-year-old man to violate the law by crossing the street against the traffic light on a variety of occasions. In half of the cases, he was dressed in a freshly pressed business suit and tie; on the other occasions, he wore a work shirt and trousers. The researchers watched from a distance and counted the number of pedestrians waiting at the corner who followed the man across the street. Like the children of Hamelin who crowded after the Pied Piper, three and a half times as many people swept into traffic behind the suited jaywalker. In this case, though, the magic came not from his pipe but his pinstripes.[32]

32 Robert B. Cialdini, Influence: *The psychology of persuasion* (Harper Collins, 1984), 227.

(**Note:** *No humans were harmed in the conduct of this experiment.)*

Isn't it amazing that US presidential candidates often wear chinos and rolled up sleeves on the campaign trail but once in office it's dark suits and bright blue or red ties? President Obama wearing a tan suit made such a stir that it has its own Wikipedia page.[33] Do a web search for "appropriate interview attire" and you're likely to see recommendations to wear a power suit. That might work well for an interview at a Wall Street investment bank but not so much for a San Francisco Bay Area tech startup.

Remember from Todorov's research that System 1 notices these markings within tens of milliseconds and System 2 makes judgments within a few hundred milliseconds more. But it goes well beyond the surface of our skin and clothes we wear. We also identify ourselves as part of a particular group by the car we drive (sedan, sports, hybrid, electric, pickup), the music we listen to (rock, jazz, reggae, classical, punk, blues), the books we read (fiction, non-fiction, biopics, comics), our alma mater, birthplace, and, perhaps most curiously, by such trivialities as our preferred James Bond actor (of course with my last name, it has to be Connery), and computer operating system (remember the "I'm a Mac and I'm a PC" ads of the mid 2000s)? While a talk show host might ask their celebrity guest "Beyonce or Swift," we STEM educated inquire "Linux or Windows."

This is what makes us uniquely human. Our identity is a product of literally hundreds of different attributes such that it is mathematically improbable to ever have a truly identical twin.

STORY TIME WITH GOLDY

If you're going to have Sierra Hotel aircraft flown by Sierra Hotel Mavericks on big ass Navy carriers, somebody has to be in charge of designing and developing the aircraft and its weapons. In the Navy, that responsibility resides with the Naval Air Systems Command—NAVAIR. NAVAIR has two primary divisions—Aircraft Division located at NAS Patuxent River, Maryland, and Weapons Division at NAS China Lake, California. If you want to do business as a contractor with Pax River, you had better be dressed in a suit and tie

33 https://en.wikipedia.org/wiki/Obama_tan_suit_controversy

for every meeting with government personnel. Otherwise, you won't be respected. Conversely, when visiting China Lake, a suit and tie is treated skeptically, equivalent to the indignity bestowed on used car salesmen.

Don't ask me how I know this—just take my word for it.

Dress at or slightly above the level of your audience when presenting under normal circumstances. Too casual and it comes off as disrespectful. Too formal and it makes them suspicious. Of course, there are exceptions. Steve Jobs and Mark Zuckerberg had their signature casual attire no matter the occasion while John Wick always wears a black suit and tie to his assassinations.

E FOR EPOCH

Even though I saved this attribute for last, biologically speaking, the very first thing we notice about somebody is their relative age. Not at the granular level of number of birthdays but more along generational lines starting with "cutie pies."

Huh?

Researchers have been wondering how we humans define cute and why we almost universally consider babies to be cute (even when they aren't). What about someone's looks makes us coo "Ahh, look at how cute they are?" Researchers considered facial features, attire, hair style, all manner of explanations and eventually settled on the ratio of head size to body size.

WTF?

Yep.

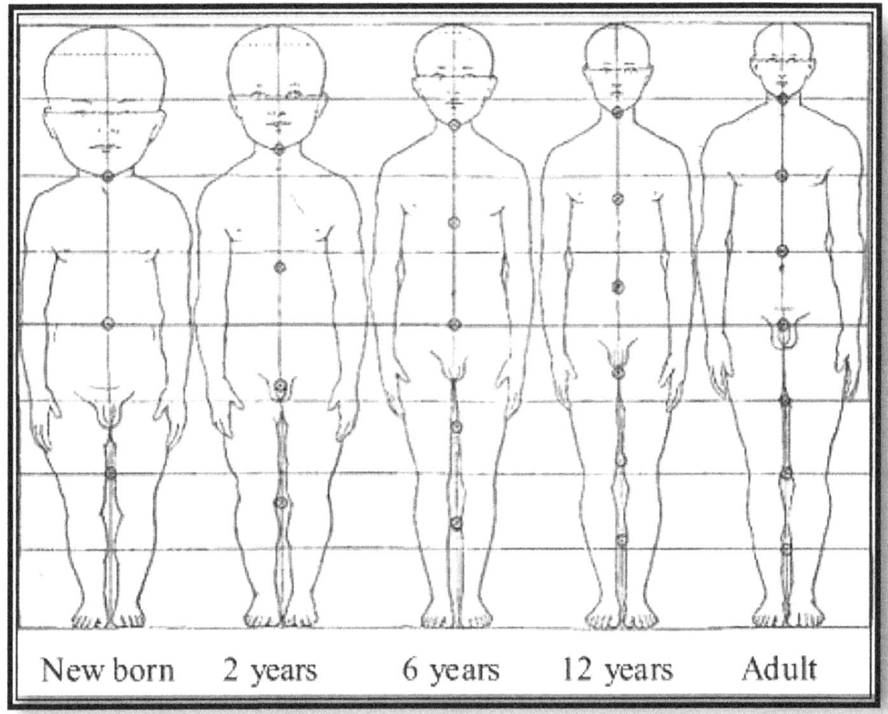

FIGURE 4 — WOULD SOMEBODY PLEASE GET SOME CLOTHES ON THESE PEOPLE![34]

What you may not have consciously realized is that at birth, the human head (and many animal species) is rather large compared to body length (also true for many mammals)—one-quarter, in the case of a human infant. An adult's head is only one-eighth the length of the body (Figure 4). It is speculated that the "cuteness" factor of an oversized head helped inspire the "it-takes-a-village-to-raise-a-child" response. In other words, judging a baby as cute helped ensure nourishment and protection (what scientists call nurturant feelings) would be forthcoming from all adults in the tribe, not just the parents.

This may explain why in 1996, female gorilla Binti Jua from the Brookfield Zoo in Illinois cradled a three-year-old human boy who had accidentally fallen fifteen feet into the gorilla enclosure, eventually carrying

---

34 Illustration from P.H. Morris, V. Reddy and R.C. Bunting, "The survival of the cutest: who's responsible for the evolution of the teddy bear?" in *Animal Behaviour,* 50(6), 1995, 1697-1700.

the boy over to paramedics. The story is just too amazing not to see for yourself: https://youtube.com/watch?v=puFCuMac0Vk

Yes, I know we're not presenting to babies. I am merely pointing out that you are likely to quickly recognize the rough epoch (generation) of your listener as being of your own or not. Of course, that immediately sets into motion the Us versus Them (Baby Boomer versus Millennial, or whatever) biases. For example, a Baby Boomer like me, presenting to an audience full of Millennials will be faced with several challenges, not the least of which is the use of my outdated pop culture references. I mentioned that I have been working on this book for a long time. I even coined the title "Tell It Like a TOPGUN" a decade ago, long before there was a hint of a sequel. With more than thirty years having passed since the original movie's release, I came across more and more young adults who, even if they had heard of it, never saw it. Fortunately, with the sequel's release, many have opted to watch the original.

Throughout my early working career in the aerospace and defense industry I dealt with one generation of listener—Boomers like me (Us). By the time I graduated college the Greatest Generation had retired, and the Gen X crowd didn't start working until 2000. Now, two decades later, we have nearly four distinct generations in the workplace with varying styles as lovingly illustrated in Figure 5.

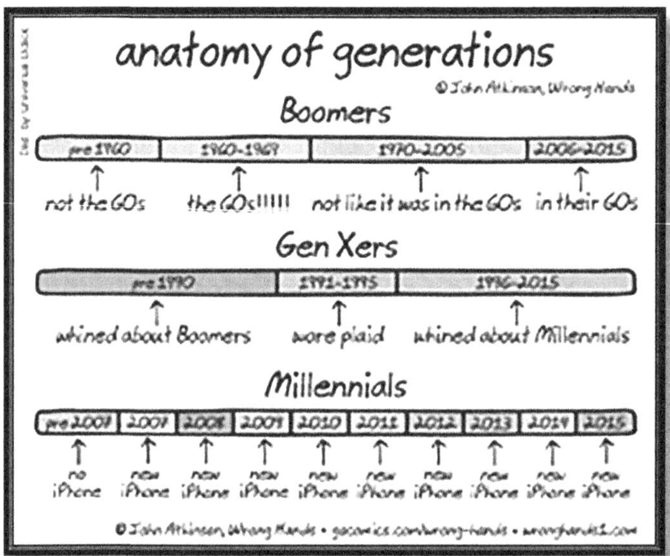

FIGURE 5 — SO TRUE.[35]

All kidding aside, our Epoch affects many aspects of our decision making. Neuroscientists will tell you that our System 2 decision-making skills, more formally our pre-frontal cortex (PFC), the seat of executive function, is not fully formed until we reach 25 (give or take a few years, and males later than females). This is precisely why your auto insurance premiums dropped significantly when you turned 25 and rental car agencies won't rent to drivers younger than that. From the statistics of millions of data points, they both know that we're safer above that age. Neuroscientists now know the reason why.

STORY TIME WITH GOLDY

Back in the late 90s, the "Dot Com" epoch, I was an instructor at the Naval Postgraduate School, in Monterey, California, teaching military aircraft accident investigation and prevention techniques. I had been given permission to consult to a Bay Area gaming company

35 Illustration from https://wronghands1.com/ © John Atkinson.

(whose name you would recognize today as an industry leader) that wanted to develop a computer flight simulator that replicated the training path that Marine helicopter pilots experience (think Call of Duty for jarhead rotorheads). We had recently finished our first milestone and needed to brief the "Big Man" at Sony gaming HQ (oops, did I just say that out loud?) to get approval for our next slug of funding (a Scenario 4 Persuade the PM situation).

The three of us dutifully put on our suits and ties and drove up to San Mateo. Being escorted into the conference room, all three of us Baby Boomers, looked around and quickly realized we were waaaaaay overdressed. The "Big Man," who none of us had ever met in person, finally arrived. He couldn't have been a day over 29 and was as formally dressed as Zuckerberg, *sans* hoodie but with holes in his jeans. Whack! His first impression of us—old fogies that couldn't connect to the gaming generation—no doubt stuck in his head regardless of how well we had presented. The project was cancelled soon after.

As with the advice on Posture, start today to be an observer of Epoch. Practice it both in social and professional settings. Don't just notice the hair difference—I used to have a forehead, now it's a fivehead. Rather, notice how the different generations are culturally predisposed regarding their risk tolerance, employment loyalty, patience, etc. For example, a 65-year-old decision-maker is likely to be more risk averse than a 45-year-old because the younger one has more room to recover from failure.

As you continue the design of your presentation, make note of the Epoch you're targeting.

Summary of SPIEing on your Listeners

"If you wish to persuade me, you must think my thoughts, feelings, and speak my words."

- Marcus Tullius Cicero, 106 – 43 B.C.E.

Table 6 below lists questions to ask yourself when SPIE-ing on your proposed listener(s) so that you can use this knowledge in the design and delivery of your talk. The key strategy to consider is how to find as many common intersections as you can to maximize the Us interpretation and minimize the Them response.

Table 6 — Ethical SPIE-ing

	What you can notice when SPIE-ing on your (proposed) listener(s).
Sex	Opposite or same sex as yours? Opposite or same sexual orientation? How might you adjust your presentation accordingly?
Posture	Is their posture primarily receptive or resistant? During the presentation, notice a shift in their posture signaling trust over skepticism. Can posture help us determine who the real decision-maker is?
Identity	What's their race, religion, native language, birthplace, alma mater, favorite sports team, etc.? Are there any intersections with you? What do their markings say about their identity? How do they want to be known? Are they hiding something (covering a tattoo, dressing down or up from normal)? What might that say about their identity?

	What you can notice when SPIE-ing on your (proposed) listener(s).
Epoch	Are they your generation or not? What is the same about their generation and yours? What is different about your generation and theirs?

CATER TO THE LEFT

Imagine yourself as an army colonel on the field of battle in World War II fighting for the Allied Powers. You've been given orders to capture an enemy enclave up ahead. You are told you will have specific resources (tanks, fuel, soldiers, ammunition, etc.) but the mission must be accomplished by the end of the third day. You assemble your staff to plan out the mission. You finish the plan and are told to brief the commanding general. The most important question to ask in this moment is: "Which general am I briefing, Patton or Bradley?"

During the war, these two generals were practically polar opposites in their behavioral approach to commanding their troops. George "Blood and Guts" Patton was very much an egotist bent on succeeding at all costs. He was a big risk seeker with a perception of invincibility, with such laser focus on speed as a strategy that he once outran his supply lines, forcing him to stall his advance against the enemy.

Contrast that with Omar Bradley, the "G.I.'s General." He was given that nickname by the famous American war correspondent Ernie Pyle who observed Bradley as someone that possessed the skill of making casual conversation with the lowest-ranking solider on the battlefield as if they were hometown buddies. Bradley was also an academician and educator. He spent most of his time between the two World Wars in Army teaching posts.

Mind you, during the European Campaign, both men had risen to 3-star rank[36] so, from a presentation planning perspective, you might think

36 Patton would go on to earn his 4th star in April 1945, after his successful push into German territory. Bradley would later become the last of the 5-star officers, a rank reserved solely for wartime and bestowed sparingly on only nine men in US military history of any service.

to present them identical content. The important takeaway is to recognize that most presenters focus on what ***they want to say*** rather than what the ***audience wants (or needs) to hear.***

Political strategist Frank Luntz drives this point home in the title of his book, *Words that Work: It's not what you say, it's what people hear* that counts. In it he relates the story of how quickly the national debate about inheritance taxes shifted by changing the terminology from "Estate Tax" to "Death Tax." The word "estate" conjured visions of large country mansions with manicured lawns.

As soon as the phrase was changed to Death Tax, many more Americans realized the tax consequences related to everything they owned, including the clothes on their back at the time of demise, not just their one-room condominium in a Florida retirement village. This allowed Congress to pass legislation that changed the floor from $650,000 to a whopping $5.5M (phased in over a period of years, of course). Think about that. A single word produced a 9x multiplier.

Returning to our hypothetical WWII analogy, you must shape your presentation one way or another depending on whether your audience is Patton or Bradley. The underlying timing and strategic objectives of your mission remain unchanged.

This may seem obvious now that you've read about it, but, in my experience, this is **THE NUMBER ONE** mistake that presenters make when designing their talk. They concentrate more heavily on what they want to say and fail to consider what the listener wants to hear (yes, I'm purposefully repeating this cautionary note).

Since we're unable to have our listeners take personality surveys, brain scans, or have blood draws, I have crafted a practical method of quickly analyzing observed behavior for subjective clues that can help shape the design and delivery of your presentation. I crafted the mnemonic LEFT to help you remember the four basic behavioral types of individuals—Leaders, Egoists, Friends, and Thinkers—summarized in Table 7.

Table 7 — Look LEFT

Type	What we notice about them: Behavior, Language, Appearance (clothes, car, office, etc.)
Leader	Focused on speed of action and enterprise value. They tend to drive fast cars in the fast lane of traffic. You might spot a Tesla, Audi, BMW, Lexus, or Infiniti in their parking spot. If invited to their office you'll notice a clean and organized desk, lack of personal artifacts, and furnishings that match their status. Family photos, when present, are likely facing themselves instead of outward toward visitors. Written correspondence is typically short and replete with "we" and "us" language. Of the four types, Leaders are the most risk-seeking since they understand and accept the risk versus reward equation. Note that just because someone is in a leadership position or has leadership qualities doesn't necessarily make them a Leader type in the sense presented here. General Bradley is a classic example of someone in a leadership position who has leadership behaviors but, as Ernie Pyle noted, was far more friendly than the typical image of a wartime leader.
Egoist	Focused on self-image. They wear stylish clothes and drive fancy cars (e.g., Rolls Royce, Jaguar, Ferrari, Bugatti) but in the slow lane so they can be seen. These are the types that own a Lamborghini and live in Malibu Beach where the speed limit maxes out at 35 mph. They use the language of "me" and "I" in both written and verbal communication. They understand risk but are unwilling to accept any personal fault when something goes wrong. Stereotypical career paths include politicians, professional athletes, celebrities, and entrepreneurs. Well-known examples include Steve Jobs, Oprah Winfrey, and the 45th President of the USA. Did Jobs lead a company, Winfrey an entertainment empire, and 45 a nation? Yes, but that's not what drove them to success. Rather it was their desire to prove themselves to others.

Type	What we notice about them: Behavior, Language, Appearance (clothes, car, office, etc.)
Friend	Focused on not wanting to stand out in a crowd, these are the individuals that belong to bowling leagues, coach little league teams, and attend tailgate parties. They drive minivans and other high-occupancy vehicles so they can chauffer their friends around. They wear clothes from discount stores. They abhor risk regardless of the expected reward and they're the most loyal of the four. Their office is filled with photos of kids, grandkids, and friends. Perhaps even plants, stuffed animals, sports team memorabilia, and other Us-type artifacts thrown in for good measure. Stereotypically, these are government employees and union workers who rarely quit their jobs, get divorced, leave their church, or abandon their favorite sports team irrespective of win-loss record (shout out to my late, diehard New York Jets-loving Uncle Joseph).
Thinker	A quick glance at their office and you'll find a poster with the radiofrequency spectrum, the periodic table, or a coding process diagram on the wall. They have reference books everywhere – in bookcases, on their desk, strewn around the room on chairs, tables, and the floor. They drive the safest of cars in the middle lane of a three-lane highway just to give themselves options. They understand that all projects have risks, so they're constantly thinking of mitigation strategies. They wear functional clothing (e.g., lab coats). Fashion, hygiene, and self-care are incidental to life. Emails are lengthy—they tell you how to build the watch in addition to answering the "what time is it?" question. They're stereotypically engineers, lawyers, scientists, and accountants.

Table 8 shares my assessments of some well-known pop culture characters.

Table 8 - Art Imitates Life

TV Series	Leader	Ego	Friend	Thinker
The Office (US)	Andy	Michael	Jim	Dwight
Ted Lasso	Roy	Jamie	Ted	Coach Beard
Suits	Rebecca	Harvey	Rachel	Mike

Before going any further, I do not want you to make any judgment about which LEFT type is "better" or "worse" than the other. The world needs all of them. As you read through the description of each, you likely found yourself in one or more of the boxes. Instead of bemoaning where you would like to be, celebrate your ability to recognize who you are. As for me, I am self-aware enough to know that my ego is the primary driver in my life. Fortunately for me, my family recognizes and accepts this situation, for which I am grateful.

Table 9 provides a summary of the easily noticed characteristics that can help you tune your "Spidey-Sense" to profile your anticipated listener (or colleague, boss, cousin, whatever).

Table 9 — Snapshot of Looking to the LEFT

	Dress	Car	Office	Favorite App	Risk Tolerance	Sport
Leader	Custom-tailored	Fast car in the Fast Lane	Clean & organized	Data Science Dashboards	High	Individual
Egoist	Luxury Brands	Stylish Car in the slow Lane	Stylish	Social Media	No Fault	Key-man positions
Friend	Discount Store	Minivan	Pictures of family & friends; plants; knickknacks	Email	Very Low	Team sports
Thinker	Functional	Safe	Disorganized but Functional	CAD/CAM, Spreadsheets	Mitigated	Chess

Think of a colleague (peer, superior or subordinate) you interact with frequently. In Figure 6 below, use a symbol (□) to represent your assessment of your colleague on a scale from 1 to10 for each of the four LEFT attributes. Use a different symbol (O) to represent your self-assessment.

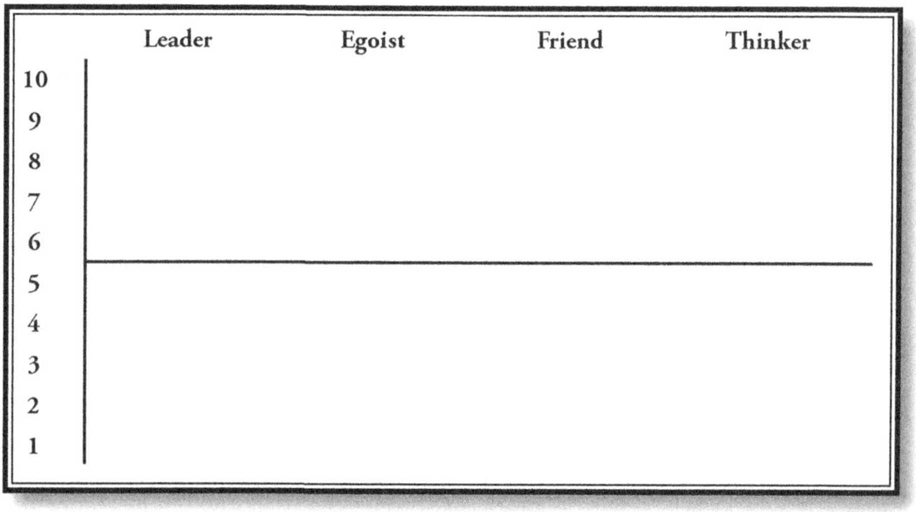

Leader Egoist Friend Thinker

10
9
8
7
6
5
4
3
2
1

Figure 6 — Charting the LEFT

Figure 7 is an example from my own life. This is a grounded assessment of me and one of my partners in an ill-advised nightclub investment. Can you guess by now whether I'm the circle or the square?

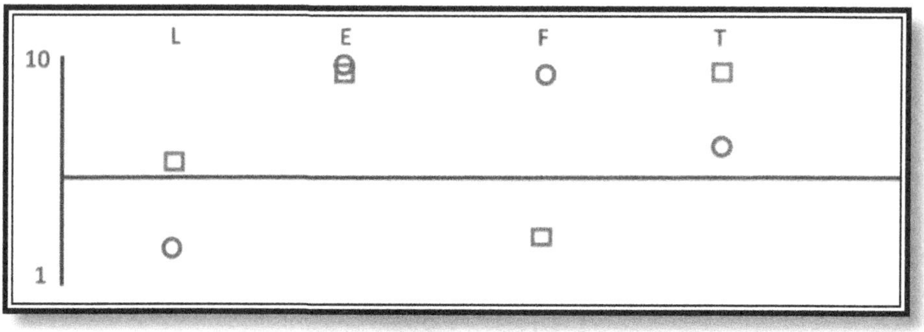

L E F T

10

1

Figure 7 — The author and one his former business partners.

Here is what to notice as you imagine comparing yourself to another.

First, it's rare to exhibit just one of the four traits. As you can see in Figure 7 most of us are above the middle line on at least two of them. (I'm the square, and my former business partner is the circle).

Second, there are some attributes that are more compatible than others. For example, Leader, Friend, and Thinker types prefer working with their same type while Egoists rarely get along with other Egoists. My partner Tony and I learned how to effectively deal with this situation by always trying to out-compliment the other in front of crowds. This stroked both our egos while also establishing a certain pedigree for prospects and customers.

Third, don't conflate somebody's position with their LEFT type. Steve Jobs led Apple to become the most valuable company on the planet, but he didn't actually care about being a leader. Since his death and the publication of both authorized and unauthorized biographies, we now know that Jobs was a rather cruel boss, driving many employees, including his partner Steve Wozniak, to quit rather than endure his abuse. He wanted his company to create life-changing products for worldwide adoption, but most importantly he wanted everyone to know that he was responsible for his company's success.

Similarly, while General Bradley certainly held many high-ranking leadership positions, his motivation was the undying care for the troops under his command. Ironically, in a post-war study, it appears that Bradley's aversion to risk led to more casualties among his forces than those of "Blood and Guts" Patton.

Practice graphing LEFT as often as possible. Now that you know how to notice, observe, and assess the four basic behavioral types of humans, you need to consider that information in the design of your presentation as advised in Table 10 below.

Table 10 — Cater to the LEFT

Type	Strategies for Presenting
Leader	Make it short: 5 minutes or less, with 10 to 15 minutes available for discussion. Focus on speed of action and enterprise value. Contrast the risk vs. the reward if successful.
Egoist	Focus on how your idea or project will enhance the listener's identity. Ensure the Egoist will never be blamed for any project failures.
Friend	The more meetings the better. Avoid as much risk as possible. Like the Egoist, but for a different psychological reason, avoid putting the Friend's identity at stake.
Thinker	Focus on making well-grounded assessments. Use 3 (or more) pieces of evidence for each claim. Highlight all significant risks and risk mitigation measures.

To put a cap on this module, I'll share two stories.

Here's a real-world example from Professor Emeritus of Psychology and Marketing at Arizona State University, Robert Cialdini. His work involved observing the most influential members of various industries. In one example, he was hired as a busboy at a restaurant (his doctoral degree left him underqualified to be a waiter) which proved to be a fortuitous way of surreptitiously noticing the work habits of the establishment's best waiter.

> So I began to linger in my duties around Vincent's tables to observe his style. I quickly learned that his style was to have no single style. He had a repertoire of them, each ready to be called on under the appropriate circumstances. When the customers

> were a family, he was effervescent—even slightly clownish—directing his remarks as often to the children as to the adults. With a young couple on a date, he became formal and a bit imperious in an attempt to intimidate the young man (to whom he spoke exclusively) into ordering and tipping lavishly. With an older, married couple, he retained the formality but dropped the superior air in favor of a respectful orientation to both members of the couple. Should the patron be dining alone, Vincent selected a friendly demeanor—cordial, conversational, and warm.[37]

Some of you might interpret Vincent's behavior as being inauthentic. That of a chameleon willing to change his personality as soon as he sniffs the odor of a bigger tip. My view is that he's an extremely caring service provider. Someone willing to put his own behavioral style aside for the sake of his customer.

In the highly entertaining series *Ted Lasso*, the Ted character takes one of his distraught football (a.k.a. soccer in less sophisticated circles) players aside after missing a crucial play in practice:

Ted: *Do you know what the happiest animal on earth is?*

Sam: *Uh, no.*

Ted: *Goldfish. Know why?*

Sam: *No.*

Ted: *Because they have a ten-second memory. Be a goldfish Sam.*

I say: "Be a Vincent!"

---

37 Cialdini, *Influence*, 233.

STORY TIME WITH GOLDY

For Doc's eulogy, and for "Inform the Industry" type talks in general, you can assume that there will be a sprinkling of all four types in the room. But since my primary listeners were his immediate family members and a few especially close friends, I wanted to cater to their individual needs.

- Retired judge father: Thinker | Friend.
- Traditional mother: Friend.
- Accountant brother: Thinker | Egoist.
- Retired 3-star Admiral that helped him get into pilot training: Leader | Friend.
- Real estate lender neighbor: Friend | Egoist
- Former housemate: Friend | Thinker

I made notes of all the key audience members and made sure various portions of my talk would be specifically catered to their individual LEFT listening.

RISKY BUSINESS

The marketing poster for another widely-acclaimed Tom Cruise movie that's *not Top Gun*, uses the teaser line, "There's a time for playing it safe and a time for *Risky Business*"[38]—a truism of basic human nature.

Influenced by both nature and nurture, we can divide the human population (and most mammalian populations) into two distinct camps—risk seekers and risk avoiders—based on complex wiring and signaling in our brains. The circuit responsible for this polarity is, once again, our PFC, just behind our forehead,[39] which compares the levels of two signals

38 1983's Risky Business was both a critical and financial success for the younger Tom Cruise earning over $60 million at the box office on a production budget one tenth the size ($6M).

39 For the purist, we're referring to a specific area of the PFC called the ventromedial prefrontal cortex (vmPFC) situated just above the eyes.

projecting from the brain's limbic region—dopamine produced by the ventral tegmental area (VTA) in Figure 8 and epinephrine produced by the amygdala (AMY) (an oversimplistic explanation, for sure). It is important to understand that the two are in a constant state of "risk versus reward" tension when it comes to your listener's decision-making process.

"Do I risk spending our company's money on the unproven product he just presented?"

"What's the reward if it works as advertised?"

"If the results she just presented are true, shouldn't we adopt the new process immediately?

"What risks are we overlooking?"

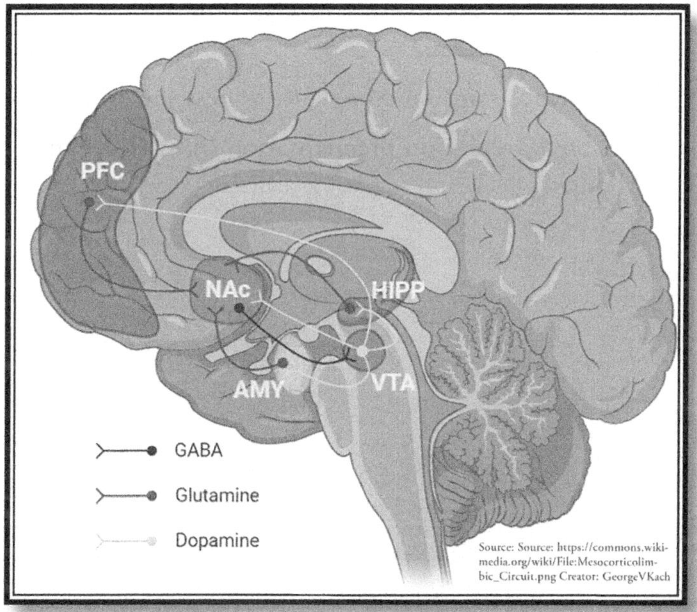

FIGURE 8 – BRAIN AREAS INVOLVED IN RISK / REWARD SENSITIVITY

As a presenter, it's your obligation to uncover your listener(s) risk tolerance and adjust your presentation accordingly. You can make some preliminary assessments based on some of the biological underpinnings you learned from our System 1 exploration. For example, due to the influence of testosterone, men are more risk-seeking than women—General George Patton, Chuck Yeager, Steve Jobs, Alex Honnold, and Elon Musk are well-known modern examples. But this is not a universal truth—witness Madame Marie Curie, Amelia Earhart, Joan Rivers, and Malala Yousafzai.

Interesting story about Honnold, or as some like to jokingly refer to him from his solo climb up Mt. Capitan in Yosemite National Park, Alex Honnolding. Neuroscientists for years were eager to examine the fear response in his brain. Some speculated that, through some genetic defect, his amygdala was missing. In 2016, they finally got their chance, and the results were quite remarkable. Although he has all the necessary piece parts, as it turns out, there's an absence of any signaling from the amygdala to his PFC. Even more remarkable were some of the intuitively incongruent findings (Figure 9) such as:

- Well below average on the extraversion scale
- Well below average neuroticism (he doesn't brag about his accomplishments)
- Well above average on conscientiousness (he mitigates his risk)
- Well above average on premeditation (his risk-seeking is planned)

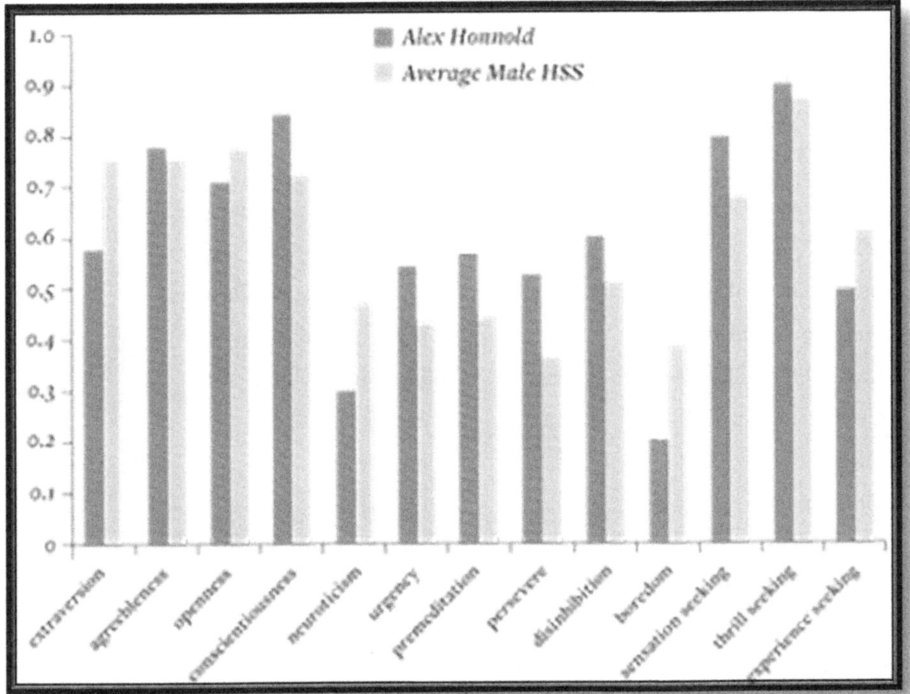

Figure 9 — Honnold's Brain is in a Free Solo Class of its Own [40]

Obviously, you won't be able to do an fMRI on your listeners, nor are you likely to ask them to fill out a risk tolerance survey (with the exception of financial advisors who often do so for new clients). So, what can you do? The politically incorrect act of profiling. Yes, I'm encouraging you to ethically profile your listeners using the LEFT and SPIE TTPs already covered. All else being equal, the following table may provide a starting point with the caveat that "your mileage may vary (Table 11)."

40 https://nautil.us/the-strange-brain-of-the-worlds-greatest-solo-climber-236051/

TABLE 11 - Profiling Risky Behavior

Risk Seekers	Risk Avoiders
Men	Women
Entrepreneurs	Union workers
Extreme sports enthusiasts	Team sports enthusiasts
Military personnel	Government civilian personnel
Investment Bankers	Accountants & Bookkeepers
Professional athletes	Healthcare professionals
Leader Types (LEFT scale)	Friend Types (LEFT scale)
Celebrities (actors, athletes)	Lawyers
Pilots	Engineers
First responders	Teachers
US citizens	European & Asian citizens
Salesmen	Contracts Officers

STEP 2 REVIEW

In this module, we covered the following topics:

- Triune Brain Theory: Stem (Croc), Limbic (Emotions), Neo-Cortex (Rationality)
- System 1 (automatic, fast, parallel processing) and System 2 (slow, thoughtful, serial processing) brain
- Us (in group) vs. Them (out group)
- **SPIE**ing on your Listener(s)
    - Sex
    - Posture
    - Identity
    - Epoch
- **Cater to the LEFT**
    - Leaders
    - Egoists
    - Friends
    - Thinkers
- **Risk Tolerance**

MAKE IT PERSONAL CHECKLIST

MAKE IT PERSONAL

1. SPIE .... PROFILE

NOTE

Use their social media, "About" pages on websites, curriculum vitae (C.V.), and official biographies (most VIPs will provide them in advance). You can also interview colleagues and assistants for clues. These same tools can and should also be used in item 4 of this checklist, Cater to the LEFT.

2. US vs. THEM .... SELECT A CONNECTION
3. US anecdote .... DESIGN

WARNING

Under no circumstances should you be disingenuous or design a flimsy connection ("Oh, wow, my 3rd cousin once removed grew up 150 miles from where you spent the summer before 9th grade"). This can immediately trigger the slimy-car-salesman-anaphylactic-shock response.

4. Cater to the LEFT .... GRAPH YOU AND THEM

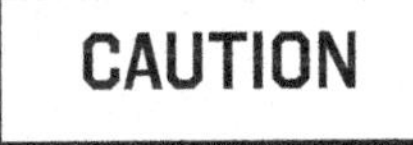

Be sure to avoid behavioral conflicts such as an Egoist presenting to another Egoist. Be a Vincent.

5. Risk tolerance .... PROFILE
6. Speech Acts .... CHECK
   a. ASSERTIONS are true and sincere
   b. ASSESSMENTS are grounded by factual assertions
   c. DECLARATIONS are fully described

STEP 3: MAKE IT EMOTIONAL

It's just emotion that's taken me over.

- Barry and Robin Gibb

We are not thinking machines that feel, rather, we are feeling machines that think.

- Neuroscientist Antonio Damasio

A TALE OF TWO CHICKENS

Recall that in MacLean's Triune Brain Theory, besides automated functions like breathing, our reptilian brain cares solely about the 3 Fs: food, fighting, and fornicating. One of the positive side effects of the evolution of our limbic brain is the emergence of emotions. There's wide recognition among social scientists that we exhibit six basic feelings: sadness, happiness, fear, anger, surprise, and disgust. This is not purely a human trait but one that is largely shared across the mammalian kingdom. Scientists have observed:

- herds of elephants mourning the death of a herd member
- lions expressing joy when being reunited with their human caretakers
- cats that fear water
- angry mama bears protecting their cubs
- using surprise to condition animal behavior
- chimps that avoid or delay eating disgusting food[41]

41 Cecile Sarabian, Barthelemy Ngoubangoye and Andrew J. J. MacIntosh, *"Avoidance of biological contaminants through sight, smell and touch in chimpanzees"* in Royal Society Open Science, 4(11), 2017, 170968.

Two hundred million years of mammalian evolution guarantee that emotions play a very large part in both animal and human decision-making.

In the acknowledgements of this book, I thanked my Shotokan Karate Sensei Shojiro Sugiyama for his teachings. One of the most memorable introductory talks he gave to new students is the difference between self-defense and martial arts.

He tells the story of growing up in rural Japan with a chicken coop in the backyard. Just about every day, he would look outside and see one of his chickens running away from the neighborhood feral cat. One day, he looked outside and saw the chicken chasing the cat. He discovered that protecting her newly hatched chicks gave her the courage to challenge the cat's dominance. In other words, martial artists find increased emotional fortitude in the protection of others over themselves.

These observations and anecdotes have led researchers (including Nobel laureates) to the near universal agreement among us that we humans make our decisions emotionally first and then rationalize the choice afterwards. The common narrative that emotional individuals cannot make rational decisions was upended by Portuguese-American neuroscientist Antonio Damasio. His research focused on individuals who had suffered permanent damage (tumors, strokes, injuries) to the emotional centers of their brains. The results showed that such patients were largely unable to make any decisions at all because of "paralysis by analysis."[42] Put simply, no matter how much information we have, we eventually rely on gut instinct.

Other studies confirm this.[43] Researchers from the McCombs School of Business in Austin, Texas, studied what they called "post-hoc rationalization," which also concluded that we make decisions emotionally first and then rationalize. The following comes from an article published by the school summarizing the researchers' findings, cheekily titled "A Tale of Two Chickens."

> McCombs marketing professor Raj Raghunathan and PhD student Szu-Chi Huang point to their research study that shows

42 Bechara, A., Damasio, H., & Damasio, A. R. (2000). "Emotion, decision making and the orbitofrontal cortex." *Cerebral cortex,* 10(3), 295-307.

43 https://www.psychologytoday.com/us/blog/feeling-smart/201502/why-our-emotions-are-more-rational-we-think

> comparative features are important, but mostly as justification after a buyer makes a decision based on emotional response.
>
> In one phase of their study, Raghunathan and Huang showed participants two photos. One was a nice looking, plump chicken. The other was a chicken that looked thin and sickly. Participants were told that the plump chicken was a natural chicken, and the thin chicken was genetically engineered.
>
> The researchers informed half of the participants that natural chickens were healthy but less tasty, and genetically engineered chickens were tasty but less healthy. The other half were told the opposite.
>
> Overwhelmingly, sets of participants expressed a preference for the nice plump chicken, but their justifications were different. The first group claimed it was because they valued health above taste, and the second group said it was because the taste was more important. Neither group seemed to justify their choice based on how they felt about the chicken's looks. They felt compelled to justify their emotional choices with non-emotional reasons, to the point that the two groups found completely opposite ways to justify the same decision."[44]

To further drive this lone data point home, think about restaurant menus of late. In the craze to cater to healthier eating, many restaurants now either have a dedicated healthy choice section or put an icon next to the choices that have fewer calories. Non-scientifically, you can make a fairly accurate guess that only 20-30% of such items on a menu belong to that category. In other words, about 30% of consumers prefer healthy eating (vast oversimplification, of course, but useful for our purposes here).

This implies that in the McCombs chicken survey, roughly 30% of each group should've chosen the healthier chicken meat regardless of its looks. But that's not what happened. Their visual system produced a disgust response for one of the two chickens, manipulating the participant to adjust their preference.

---

44 McCombs Today."Do you make buying decisions based on logic or emotion? A tale of two chickens". McCombs School of Business" at http://mccombstoday.org/2010-04-do-you-make-buying-decisions-based-on-logic-or-emotion-a-tale-of-two-chickens/

Now let's take a dive into the deep recesses of the limbic system to learn how to ethically manipulate our listeners' emotions to drive their decision making.

HI-HO THE DERRY-O, A **DOSE**-ING WE WILL GO

Recalling the discussion about Kahneman's System 1, this module will make you aware of four key neurotransmitters produced in our limbic system that drive decision-making and memorability (more on that second aspect later). Recall that our limbic system is, evolutionarily speaking, very old, dating back to our mammalian roots tens of millions of years ago. In other words, if you're looking for the so-called animal instinct that drives business decision-making, start here. Each of the four chemicals cited below are essential to daily life and the overproduction or underproduction of each are largely responsible for many mental health imbalances such as depression, addiction, and attention deficit hyperactivity disorder (ADHD).

As the subtitle of this section implies, I coined the mnemonic DOSE as the contextual tool to help you recall these four specific brain chemicals vying for attention in System 1.

D FOR DOPAMINE

This is the reward drug and why we get out of bed each day.[45] Produced in the striatum and nucleus accumbens and projected to the prefrontal cortex, the locus of "executive function" in our brain, dopamine is tied to desire. Imagine our hominid ancestor spotting an apple tree in the distance. After walking towards the tree, she suddenly realizes that she has closed half the distance. A rush of dopamine releases to motivate her to continue walking towards the tree. Biologists and neuroscientists used to believe that dopamine was triggered only **after** accomplishing a task. However, they have since discovered that a bigger dose is triggered from the mere anticipation of reward. In other words, we care more about chasing the prize than actually catching it. And yes, many sex therapists agree on this as a contributing factor to extramarital affairs.

While dopamine is essential to being a productive member of society, it has its dark side. Our brains are addicted to dopamine production. Again,

45 R. A. Wise, "Dopamine, learning and motivation" in *Nature reviews neuroscience,* 5(6), 2004, 483-494.

that's why we get out of bed in the morning to chase that higher grade in school, a raise at work, a winning goal in sports, or the Nobel Prize. Because it's addictive, it leads to destructive behaviors such as excessive gambling, sex addiction, extreme sports, and illicit drug use. But that shouldn't scare you away from understanding the role of dopamine and your ability to ethically manipulate it as part of the design of your presentation.

Being fully transparent, as someone who was diagnosed with ADHD just a few years ago, I discovered through both a personality test (Neurocolor®) and DNA testing (Genomind) that I have an issue with dopamine processing in my brain. Specifically, I reuptake it too quickly (burn it off) so I'm constantly seeking activities that produce more dopamine. Writing this book has been a big help since I get a boost with every page. However, it also means that it has been difficult to stay focused on its completion.

All else being equal, the presenter who can produce more dopamine in their listeners will produce a more favorable outcome.

Start making a list of various rewards your listener(s) can anticipate if they "buy" the idea that your presentation is selling.

O FOR OXYTOCIN

This is the love drug. It is what makes us social animals, and how we learn to trust each other.[46] Our first exposure to this wonderful chemical occurs when we're placed on our mother's belly after birth. Both mother and baby are flooded with oxytocin during breastfeeding. Research shows that infants who don't receive loving strokes in their earliest days and weeks are doomed to lifelong struggles with pair bonding. As can be seen in many nature documentaries, it doesn't even have to be the same species that offers this touch. Abandoned wild animals that are cared for by humans receive sufficient oxytocin to replace what they would've received from their biological parent.

---

46 Paul J. Zak, *The moral molecule: The source of love and prosperity.* (Random House, 2012).

Hug a loved one, pet your dog, high five your mate after your favorite team just scored a goal, boom, a little squirt of oxytocin. But we don't need physical touch to produce the effect. Merely thinking fondly of your spouse (assuming you're in a loving relationship, of course) produces the same effect. Our brains cannot distinguish reality from fantasy. Our neurons are merely responding to stimulus whether somatosensory (touch), visually, orally, or olfactory. This is why we cry at sentimental movies, smile when we hear our favorite teenage make-out song, and have that flash of our grandmother's face whenever we smell warm cookies. What Zak calls "reactions at a distance" are equally stimulating to our oxytocin response system and can be ethically manipulated just the same.

From this day to the ending of the world, But we in it shall be remembered; We few, we happy few, we band of brothers. - St Crispin's Day speech, King Henry, Act 4

by William Shakespeare

TOPGUN instructors are effective because of this "Band of Brothers" effect that oxytocin has among fellow warriors. You'll recall that earlier I explained that they even call each other Bro. The same effect is seen among firefighters, law enforcement officers, college fraternity and sorority brothers and sisters, religious affiliations, geographic orientation, sports team fans, etc.

This is the Us versus Them effect I wrote about earlier.

Why does this matter?

Cialdini and others have shown that we will grant trust to a stranger for no better reason than they grew up in the same neighborhood/state/country, speak the same language, went to the same college, are fans of the same ball club, once worked at the same company, or any other random connection. Because they're an Us.

This is why that car salesperson (one of the least trustworthy of professions[47]) asks a lot of personal questions when first meeting you on the showroom floor. They're looking for an Us connection.

"Oh, you grew up in Jersey, my brother lives there."

This is also why politicians work hard to prove that no matter how out of touch they might be once elected, while running for office they focus on how they come from the same hard scrabble background as you and/or your parents.

Same advice as for dopamine. All else being equal, the presenter who can produce a larger oxytocin effect will have a higher probability of producing a "yes" response from their listener.

What images and/or language might you be able to use in your presentation to produce an oxytocin connection with your listeners.

S FOR SEROTONIN

This is the mood and leadership drug.[48] When examining wolf packs and our primate cousins (chimpanzees and orangutans), researchers discovered that having higher social status increases serotonin levels. And when a beta rose to alpha status, their serotonin levels rose accordingly. Interestingly, unlike the other three chemicals in this bunch that are most present in the brain, biologists report that nearly 70% of our serotonin production is produced in the gut.

Unlike our previous two neurotransmitters dopamine and oxytocin, the evidence for serotonin production being triggered merely by words or images is far less certain. Why it's called the leadership drug may be more

---

47 https://forbes.com/sites/niallmccarthy/2019/01/11/americas-most-least-trusted-professions-infographic/_

48 Berger, M., Gray, J. A., & Roth, B. L. (2009). "The expanded biology of serotonin." *Annual review of medicine,* 60, 355-366.

related to the need for the alpha male and female to lead the pack in killing prey or finding a watering hole rather than because Bluto stood up in front of his Delta House fraternity brothers and gave a rousing, profanity-laden leadership speech (shout out to Animal House, the most profitable comedy of all time).

For now, we'll simply use the 'S' in DOSE to remind us to deal with both our own and our listener's mood. I'll have more to say about moods in a dedicated section on observing, assessing, and orchestrating receptive moods when we explore System 2 later.

E FOR EPINEPHRINE

This is the fear and arousal drug.[49] Whenever our brain observes something it doesn't recognize or recognizes as dangerous, the amygdala squirts epinephrine (and some other chemicals) to alert the body. Key physiological responses include increased heart rate, decreased blood flow to non-essential activities such as digestion and reproduction, pupil dilation, and enhanced hearing response, among the more obvious.

This is a basic survival instinct. Professional venture capital fund raiser Oren Klaff recommends beginning every presentation with something threatening precisely to promote the fear response and awaken the audience.[50] The subtle point being conveyed at the start of his presentations is: "If you don't accept my recommended solution, your problems are only going to get worse."

We can see this manipulation in political speech. The candidate starts out every speech by explaining how terrible life is or will be if you elect their opponent. The current office holder explains how voting in support of the opposition's proposed bill will destroy the world as we know it. Fear is a powerful driver of action.

Like dopamine and oxytocin, epinephrine also causes action at a distance and can be manipulated merely by thinking bad thoughts. Have you ever received that call in the middle of the night? Or, as happened to me upon walking into the Ready Room after a mission, the duty officer said, "Goldy, go see the Skipper."

---

49 Sapolsky, 2017.

50 Oren Klaff, *Pitch Anything.* (McGraw-Hill Professional Publishing, 2011).

Even before you answer the phone, or head down the carrier's passageway to your commanding officer's stateroom, your amygdala is firing on all cylinders imagining you're about to be told that someone you care about has been in a car accident or died in their sleep. But unlike the other two brain chemicals, more is not better. While Klaff is correct in that a little bit is useful to wake up the brain, too much will scare away your listener from wanting to work with you, so sprinkle it sparingly in your presentation.

As an aside, epinephrine is more commonly known as adrenaline. However, I couldn't come up with a catchier, learning-worthy mnemonic than DOSEing had I used 'A' instead of 'E'. (That's my ethical manipulation of your recall ability.)

Write down at least one fear-based consequence to include in your presentation. Here are some example ideas (not all inclusive) to imply that if the customer doesn't choose your approach they will suffer the consequences of:

- increased cost
- decreased performance
- schedule delay
- physical harm
- emotional harm
- career harm
- hair loss

SUMMARY OF DOSEING

Your takeaway from this section is to remember that our automatic reactions are heavily influenced by the relative production, circulation, and reuptake (absorption) of each of these four chemicals: dopamine, oxytocin, serotonin, and epinephrine.

Table 12 provides a list of DOSEing strategies:

Table 12 — Strategies for DOSEing your Presentation

Type	Strategies for Production
Dopamine	List the specific outcome you, your project, or your idea intends to produce. Indicate specific milestone events with dates. Use interim events along the way for projects that are lengthy. Leader types want to see speed of action and increased enterprise value. Ego types want to know how this will enhance their identity.
Oxytocin	List who else from their "tribe" is doing the same thing. Friend types want to know how this will increase their circle of friends. They also want to see lots of group gatherings as part of the project (video conferences, team meetings, social events).
Serotonin	Focus on fairness, both positive and negative (eye-for-an-eye), cooperation, and harm aversion.
Epinephrine	Produce a small bit of fear at the start of the presentation to "wake up" the brain. Cite the consequences of not following your recommendation. Too much fear might cause the listener to pull back and avoid deciding (hence the reason many climate change presentations fail to produce action).

STORY TIME WITH GOLDY

For Doc's eulogy, here's how I dealt with DOSEing (refer to the line numbers in Part 3f).

- Dopamine:
  - The joke I used at the opening about shrinking my speech down to index cards lets them know this won't be excessively long, a reward for sitting quietly in their seats.
  - Lines 76 – 82: The reward of helping a young kid in high school.
  - Lines 115 – 117: The reward of getting back into spaceflight.
- Oxytocin:
  - Lines 10 – 11: Who hasn't seen *The Wizard of Oz*? We're now all immediately connected to Us.
  - Line 23: I knew there would be a handful of doctors from his medical school days.
  - Lines 25 – 26: Appealing to the other carrier pilots and NFOs present.
  - Lines 48 – 53: Enlarging the Band of Brothers effect to the entire room.
  - Notice throughout the eulogy, I mention as many of Doc's friends as possible to make sure they all receive a dose of the love drug.
- Serotonin:
  - The entire eulogy is one large orchestration of moods.
  - The opening joke shifted the mood from somber to uplifting.
  - All the examples of how Doc helped others were designed to produce a mood of ambition and resolution to emulate his altruistic actions.
- Epinephrine:
  - Lines 7 – 11: The fear of doctor visits.

In Part 3c Best of the Best, I have picked my three favorite presentations that most succinctly demonstrate how to Tell It Like a TOPGUN. Two from US presidents – Abraham Lincoln and John F. Kennedy – and the 3rd by the master salesman himself, Steve Jobs. For now, I just want to focus on Kennedy.

In September 1962, then President Kennedy delivered what many refer to as the "Moon Speech" to a large audience at Rice University stadium in Texas. The speech is about 18 minutes and you can easily find it online. Before reading any further, take the time to watch the full video and think about how he was able to DOSE his audience. Then continue reading this book as I share a few of my observations.

Here are just a handful of the DOSEing elements the writers used in the speech.

- Dopamine:
  - Throughout the speech, he talks about all the rewards that the university, the city of Houston, and the country will reap by going to the moon including jobs, scientific discovery, and demonstration of the peaceful exploration of space.
- Oxytocin:
  - "Why does Rice play Texas?" This is one of the most brilliant lines in the speech. This was a reference to Rice, an unranked college football team and University of Texas, a top-ranked team. This produced a huge round of **Us** applause from the audience.
- Seratonin:
  - The entire theme of the speech is about setting the moods of ambition, resolution, and leadership. Quoting George Mallory's famous line about conquering Mount Everest reminds the audience that the U.S. is a world leader.
- Epinephrine:
  - Pointing out the courage that will be needed to overcome the adversity ahead.

I encourage you to read it for yourself to see if you can pick out any others.

Write at least one idea for each of the four DOSEing chemicals to include in the design of your presentation.

TO JOKE OR NOT TO JOKE; THAT IS THE QUESTION

As a survival mechanism, fear and pain is memory reinforcing. If our hominid ancestor watched a friend get skewered at a watering hole by a lion, they'd be more careful the next time. Put your hand on a hot stove as a toddler and you won't ever do that again. The flipside is also true. When we enjoy what we're doing, this too reinforces memories. While the neurotransmitters are different (see prior section), their result in the hippocampus is the same—reinforcement of the experience.

This has led many presentation skills trainers like me to encourage the sprinkling of humor throughout your presentation. I even know some presenters that religiously start every Inform the Industry-type presentation (Scenario 1) with a joke.

As you have read by now, I too am a big fan of humor. However, there are two warnings to heed. First, humor shouldn't be just for the sake of telling a great joke. It should tie directly to the content of your presentation and the outcome you're trying to produce. Every bit of humor I have been dusting throughout this book is purposeful. It's designed to keep you engaged with the material and to remember key learning points along the way. For example, the joke I told at the start of Dave's eulogy referenced a conversation with Dave's dad, not some unrelated anecdote.

This is where some television advertising creators go astray. For example, Super Bowl ads are often designed to be upbeat and humorous to match the occasion (except for us Jets fans who, since the 1960s, are forever in a sour mood during the playoffs). But notice how often or infrequently you remember the actual product brand or what they were advertising.

The second problem with humor is that you can't know who might be offended. If you're a professional comedian, there's an expectation that some of your jokes will be a turn off. But if you're briefing the CAG just prior to the Alpha Strike against a heavily defended target, that's probably not the time to crack a joke.

STORY TIME WITH GOLDY

Just prior to the COVID shutdown, I was asked to give a talk at an organization's monthly networking event. The dinner was held in New Jersey so imagine my joy in being able to share some of my childhood memories with the audience—promoting an Us response. I found a picture from my 1977 high school prom, complete with my off yellow, excruciatingly wide-lapeled, polyester leisure suit, topped off by my "Jewfro"—an afro-style hairdo worn by culturally envious Jewish teens pining to be a dancer on either Soul Train or Saturday Night Fever.

I've been using that Jewfro joke for decades without harm, especially now that I have a follicly-challenged fivehead (formerly a forehead). But apparently, I struck a nerve with at least one member of the audience who felt I was culturally insensitive. That's the danger of humor in a presentation—you never know when it crosses a line.

HERE A RISTIC, THERE A RISTIC, EVERYWHERE A HEURISTIC

Another key System 1 process involves our brain's reliance on heuristics—a way of thinking that relies on a "good enough" principle. When confronted with more than just a few choices and a complex weighting algorithm, our brains conserve energy and essentially make an informed guess to arrive at a sufficiently safe answer. The most common heuristic is known as confirmation bias: our propensity to favor information that confirms our preconceived notions and to dismiss counter arguments.

For example, while still on active duty in 1999, I was asked to give a presentation at an annual safety conference for the Brazilian Navy. At the time, the Brazilians were about to buy a retired aircraft carrier from France, making it the first South American nation with one. This decision had far-reaching military and political implications for the region and the Brazilian Navy was keen to accept this new responsibility. I researched the history of their decision-making process, and I realized that by observing American,

British, and French carrier activities, it would've been easy to succumb to confirmation bias, ignoring the decades of lessons learned that each country had accumulated. So, in the design of my presentation, instead of focusing on the present, I outlined key historical events that dramatically improved flying safety. My purpose for doing so was to give them an opportunity to avoid making the same mistakes, thus shortening their learning cycle.

Confirmation bias is just one of many heuristic algorithms designed to simplify decision-making under risk and uncertainty. Table 13 below is a summary analysis of the works of Nobel Laureate Richard Thaler[51] and that of Kahneman and his partner Tversky referenced earlier (System 1 and System 2).

Table 13 - Summary of Human Heuristics

Heuristic Property	System 1 Utilization	Example	How I applied it (or could have) when designing the Brazilian talk
Affinity	Having a more favorable opinion for in-group members (Us).	Even when companies create diversity hiring goals, they fail to hire more diverse candidates if the hiring managers aren't themselves diverse.	Show images of aircraft that I flew in the US military that are also flown in the Brazilian military. Wear my Navy uniform when delivering the talk.
Anchoring	Estimating numerical values can be influenced by an anchor.	"Is 65% higher or lower than the actual percentage of students that complete a 4-year degree in 6 or fewer years?" By changing the initial number to, say 85 or 35%, you will influence the average guess either higher or lower, respectively	Have a slide that shows the accident rates for various US military aircraft from the Air Force, Army and Marines. Then have them guess what the Navy accident rate is for comparable aircraft to highlight the increased risk of carrier aviation.

51 Thaler, R. H. & Sunstein, C. R. *Nudge: Improving decisions about health, wealth, and happiness.* Yale University Press, New Haven, CT, 2008.

Heuristic Property	System 1 Utilization	Example	How I applied it (or could have) when designing the Brazilian talk
Attribute Substitution	Substituting an easier question to answer than the one posed.	Electing politicians and hiring employees based on their looks rather than their accomplishments. Why killing "Bambi" is bad but killing an alligator is okay.	Remind them not to lose sight of the complexity of carrier operations. Too often, accidents are attributed to an individual (pilot or ground crew) when in reality it's a chain of small errors involving many others including managers and manufacturers
Availability	Deciding to use only the most readily available information instead of all relevant information.	Overall crime rate is down even though it appears higher because of media reports.	Analyzing safety incidents aboard an aircraft carrier means collecting a wide variety of historical data and interviews.
Confirmation	Tendency to seek and favor supporting information while ignoring counter-arguments.	Anti-vaxxers that continue to look for connections between vaccines and autism even though the original study and its author have been discredited.	Wanting to become a carrier-capable Navy may look easy but a lot of lives were lost along the way. Don't run before you can walk.
Framing	Relying on the context to inform the decision.	Medical procedures that are 95% *life-saving* are perceived as safer than those that are 5% *death-producing* even though they're statistically identical.	Instead of talking too much about carrier aviation accident rates, highlight the average number of accident-free flight hours flown by a typical squadron.

Heuristic Property	System 1 Utilization	Example	How I applied it (or could have) when designing the Brazilian talk
Loss Aversion	Caring more about not losing than about winning.	Selling a rising stock too soon or holding onto a falling stock too long.	While nobody wants to lose an aircraft or a crew member, if an accident occurs, don't shut down the program. Learn from the incident and prevent it from happening in the future.
Optimism	Overestimating the probability of future success while underestimating the probability of failure.	Overestimate our ability to pick winning stocks and underestimate the probability of a startup business success.	Don't expect to be operating the carrier at full operational capability (FOC) too soon. Double your time to FOC estimate and maybe even double it again.
Recency	We tend to overemphasize the value of the most recent information or experience.	Recent reporting about a commercial plane accident will cause us to think that plane travel is dangerous even though over the long term it's the safest way to travel.	Asking to give my presentation last or towards the end of the agenda to make my message last longer.
Recognition	Given two choices, going with what you know.	Ordering the same menu item every time you visit your favorite restaurant.	Existing TTPs for flying helicopters on Brazilian Navy ships will not necessarily work on the carrier for fixed-wing airplanes.

Understanding bia is critical to the crafting of your presentation, as will be discussed later when we get to the sections on design. For now, I want you to imagine how to ethically manipulate the subconscious biases listed in the table above to help you sell your ideas. I have already populated it with some ideas on how I could've applied it to my Brazilian safety talk. You should do the same for your presentation design.

Consider deploying at least one of the heuristic biases cited above to increase your "yes" chances. Alternatively, what information would you want to be sure to include in your presentation to overcome your listeners' heuristic biases?

"THANK YOU, SIR, MAY I HAVE ANOTHER?"

Whenever I think of the past, it brings back so many memories.

~ Comedian Steven Wright

In Part 3c, the section titled A Rose by Any Other Name, I give a history of how Navy flyboy nicknames are earned. Goldy was bestowed on me after a failed attempt at Neidermeyer, the caricature Army ROTC commander from the movie *Animal House.* As the sole ROTC graduate in my squadron, it was a natural fit but I dodged a bullet due to word length issues with the nametag. Whew!

In case you're one of the very few who have never seen the movie, one of the most memorable phrases to emerge was Kevin Bacon's line, "Thank you Sir, may I have another" as he is being paddled on his rump by Neidermeyer during a pledge hazing ceremony.

While many associate the meme solely as an artifact of the movie it too has its root from military service. While in boot camp, whenever a recruit screws something up, the drill sergeant assigns some form of physical punishment such as 20 pushups, scrubbing the floor with a toothbrush while on one's knees, etc. Whatever the form of discipline, the objective was to ignore the pain and ask for more punishment as a way of letting the Drill

Sergeant know that you're not going to surrender—not now, and definitely not in combat.

The sergeant's goal was to reinforce the learning through negative feedback. Researchers, including Kahneman, have generally concluded that we learn faster through positive feedback, but try telling that to the military. In any case, the ability to form longer lasting memories is tied directly to the emotional reactions we have in that moment.

Our mammalian brain evolved into a highly complex, three facet memory function—sensory, short-term, and long-term—that for most people only approximates what really happened. Understanding how our memory systems work together will help increase the probability that your presentation will be remembered and acted upon.

For simplicity's sake, accept that short-term memory occurs in our limbic layer (the hippocampus) and long-term memory consolidates in our neocortex. Whether short or long, researchers agree that our brains remember information longest when it's stored along with its context. For example, you probably don't remember the precise details of the ride home from work a week ago Thursday if nothing abnormal happened, yet it's highly likely you recall every detail of passing your driving test or your first car accident or the time that the wheel came off your axle a few miles down the highway on your way to that summer job at the Wisconsin Dells after having just had a flat tire repaired by a roadside mechanic who failed to fully tighten the bolts.

Yeah, that was me. Forty-two years ago, my car came to a stop while the wheel kept rolling, crossed the divider, and hit a car in the opposite lane head on. Fortunately, the other driver saw what was happening with enough warning to slow down and not get hurt. I remember the wheel bouncing up and onto the other car's hood. I can recall these details as if it happened yesterday.

> **Member, Select Committee to Investigate the January 6th Attack on the United States Congress:** *Can you recall what you said to the president as you saw the Capitol being breached?*
>
> **Testimony from White House Staffer:** *I cannot recall.*
>
> Yeah, right.

It's not just context that enhances retention but also the association of a memory with strong emotions. Feelings that are activated by your brain stem and limbic systems will improve your memory of an event. This is where entertainment in a presentation serves a purpose, by nudging at emotions to lengthen the impact of the information we're conveying. we're entertained when our emotional circuitry is firing at its strongest, whether on the upside (love, conquest, joy, laughter) or the downside (hate, loss, fear, sadness).

Enhancing memory through context and emotion makes sense from an evolutionary perspective. Millions of years ago when your hominid ancestors joined a friend down at the watering hole, if the friend was ambushed by an alligator, the amygdala's fear response amplified the memory of this event as a survival technique. Similarly, the joy they felt when they found that perfect apple tree after a days-long walk also served to reinforce the memory. We hominids are designed to remember what matters to our survival and ability to reproduce—watering holes, tasty foods, attractive sex partners, flat tire repairs, and dangerous predators (or presidents).

In the late 1800s, German psychologist Hermann Ebbinghaus studied human memory and developed his "Forgetting Curve" which predicts that, without intervention, most of us forget 70% to 80% of newly learned material within 48 hours.[52, 53] That's why I have designed this book and my courseware to emphasize the 20 – 30% I want you to be sure to remember. Towards the end of the book, I'll give you three suggestions to overcome the forgetting curve and improve your retention.

52 Ebbinghaus Urmanuskript, "Ueber das Gedächtniß". (Passau: Passavia Universitätsverlag, 1880).

53 Ebbinghaus' results were successfully replicated by J. Murre and J. Dros, "Replication and analysis of Ebbinghaus' forgetting curve" in *PloS one, 10*(7), 2015, e0120644.

MAKE IT EMOTIONAL CHECKLIST

So, here's your checklist for Step 3 of your mission:

MAKE IT EMOTIONAL

1. DOSE your design .... CHECK
2. Insert relevant humor .... AS REQUIRED
3. Heuristic biases .... ETHICALLY MANIPULATE
4. Briefing schedule .... LAUNCH LAST OR FIRST

NOTE

If you are one of a series of speakers, because of the recency heuristic, it is best to go last in the series, if possible. The next best option is the pole position. If you "kill it" coming out of the gate, it's only natural for the listener(s) to look for faults made by the remaining presenters.

5. Speech Acts .... CHECK
    a. ASSERTIONS are true and sincere
    b. ASSESSMENTS are grounded by factual assertions
    c. DECLARATIONS are described by their vows

STEP 4: MAKE IT COMPELLING

---

*"You can't make this sh*t up."*

~ Unknown

---

*"We humans make sh*t up all the time."*

~ Goldy

A TALE OF TWO SYSTEMS – SYSTEM 2

As a reminder, System 1 is our autonomous brain whose primary reactions are instinctual (food, fight, or fornicate), or emotional (sadness, happiness, fear, anger, surprise, and disgust). System 2 is our rational brain, the largest component of which is the prefrontal cortex (PFC) located just behind the eyes. This is the most recently evolved area and responsible for executive function—the purposeful algorithm that causes us to do the right thing even when it's not rewarding (such as saying no to an adulterous affair or, equally decadent, a 2nd croquembouche).

We often hear how genetically close we are to our chimpanzee cousins, on the order of 3 - 4% of our DNA. We also share many behavioral traits such as empathy, respect for elders, playfulness, compassion, and resourcefulness. It is the PFC's executive function algorithm that truly separates us from our primate relatives. The ability to organize, plan, prioritize, regulate emotions, and understand different points of view are uniquely human. In the following sections, I'll introduce you to the most relevant System 2 processes for designing and delivering compelling presentations.

Researchers generally agree that archaic *Homo sapiens* (anatomically modern humans) first appeared in the evolutionary chain some 200,000 - 300,000 years ago. For most of our time on this planet, the world was indifferent to our presence. We roamed in small bands of 100 to150 individuals, competing about on par with other hominids (Neanderthal,

Homo erectus, Denisovans) and barely outcompeting our primate cousins and other predators at the top of the food chain.

And then something "magical" happened about 70,000 years ago. Perhaps a DNA mutation, nobody knows for sure, but anthropologists now refer to it as the "cognitive revolution." Our more modern ancestors, *Homo sapiens sapiens* or "wise man", developed the ability to create fictional stories about the past, present, and future and to convey our stories through new language.

We know of this shift because artistic artifacts suddenly emerged such as cave paintings featuring mythical creatures or carvings like the Stadel-cave half-lion half-man figurine. What's fascinating to ponder is that we didn't start out with rudimentary drawings that evolved over time into complex illustrations. We went from nothing to sophisticated images overnight (in evolutionary terms, that is).

Our imaginations weren't limited to artistic endeavors. Anthropologists and historians generally agree that complex language also emerged during this period. The combination of imagination and complex language allowed humans to become the dominant species on the planet by flexibly coordinating and cooperating in large numbers. Historian Yuval Harari uses the following hypothetical examples to highlight this theory.[54]

- Bees can coordinate and cooperate in large numbers but not flexibly. For example, they can't overthrow the queen in favor of democratic rule.
- A challenger chimpanzee can overthrow the troop's alpha male chimp, but you can't fill an Olympic stadium on opening day of the games with 100,000 chimpanzees and expect calm, much less sing a country's national anthem in unison.

With these new-found linguistic and fictive capacities, we established kingdoms, built everlasting pyramids and coliseums, sculpted 8,000 Terracotta soldiers, and established an Incan Empire of ten million citizens, all without a written alphabet! In a world where we were slower than the cheetah, weaker than the baboon, and lacking the olfactory sense of a hyena, our ability to language became the "secret sauce" of our survival.

54 https://youtu.be/nzj7Wg4DAbs?si=uZ2M3UtaXrOknVI9

As one of my mentors, Toby Hecht, was fond of saying: "Fish swim. Birds fly. Humans language, to survive."

It's important to understand how much we relied on artistic content to communicate. Visualization was heavily relied upon in our evolutionary history. Just in the past year or so, researchers found markings on a 20,000-year-old cave painting hinting at graphic instructions for killing prey—much like the ones I used last week to assemble my IKEA coffee table. (No wonder it was so frustrating. The instructions were written by cavemen!) The adage "a picture is worth 1,000 words" has an evolutionary basis.

The written alphabet that we know today was invented a mere 3,500 years ago, a small fraction of the total time we modern humans have inhabited the earth. Reading and writing are difficult and need to be taught to us. According to data compiled by the OECD and UNESCO, 1.2 billion people were still illiterate at the turn of this century just 20 years ago.[55]

So, what did we do with all the speech acts (from Commander's Intent) we made up? We started creating myths—imaginative stories that allowed us to both entertain and cooperate in large numbers. Creating a compelling oral presentation is also a form of mythmaking—crafting a story, whether fictional or not, that moves your listeners to act in a coordinated fashion. So, now we're going to examine the power of such mythmaking and why myths and legends, like that of King Arthur and his Knights of the Round Table, are so enduring.

I SEE A PYRAMID IN YOUR FUTURE

Before proceeding any further, watch (or rewatch) Director Rob Reiner's 1987 cult classic *The Princess Bride.* To Tell It Like a TOPGUN requires that you become a premier storyteller. This movie provides the richest example of all the necessary narrative elements. I selected this movie because the following attributes allow you to watch it with young family members (which I highly encourage):

- Nothing offensive. No cursing, no nudity, only one scene with blood.
- Variety of characters with their eccentric traits.

55 https://ourworldindata.org/literacy

- Highly memorable plot lines.
- Relies strictly on conversational elements rather than absurd computer graphics.
- Near perfect alignment with the learning objectives of this module.

And besides, it's just great fun, with highly memorable memes. In the following sections, I'll be referencing the movie to help you understand and employ "best of the best" storytelling TTPs.

Hands down, **this is the most important module of the entire book.** Pay close attention because it has applicability across many aspects of your personal and professional life.

Most historians agree that the King Arthur of British folklore never existed. Yet dozens of stories, plays, musicals, and movies persist in gripping our imaginations for hundreds of years since the legend first surfaced. How can this be?

Neuroscientist Uri Hasson[56] and his colleagues have done studies on how our brains react to storytelling. They demonstrated two observable facts about the electrical patterns of our brain. First, in a normal resting state, our brain waves look entirely random and somewhat fingerprint-like in their uniqueness. However, when listening to a compelling story, a listener's brain waves eventually synchronize to the speaker's pattern in a process his team labeled neural entrainment.[57] In other words, we're wired for storytelling (Figure 10). This brain wave alignment significantly enhances memorability, overcoming the Forgetting Curve for days and weeks to follow. Neuroscientist Paul Zak confirmed that inspiring stories produce an oxytocin (one of our four DOSEing drugs) response as well, further reinforcing our long-term memory circuits.[58]

---

56 Uri Hasson, "Defend Your Research: I can make your brain look like mine" in *Harvard Business Review, 88*(12), 2010, 32-33.

57 This process is akin to the coupling effect studied in physics and engineering courses whereby two independently-oscillating systems that are connected to each other (e.g., by a spring) will eventually synchronize their oscillations.

58 Paul J. Zak, "Why inspiring stories make us react: The neuroscience of narrative" in *Cerebrum: the Dana forum on brain science* (Vol. 2015). Dana Foundation.

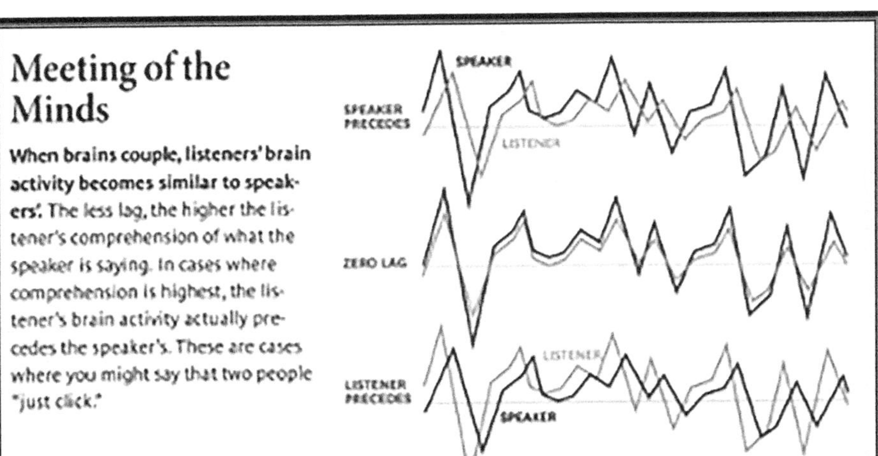

FIGURE 10 — NEURAL ENTERTAINMENT OF STORYTELLING (HASSON, 2010)

So, what makes a story compelling? How do we craft a story that increases the probability of neural entrainment?

In the late 1800s, German novelist and playwright Gustav Freytag analyzed the classics, including Homer's epic Greek poems (Illiad and Odyssey) and Shakesperean plays. Eventually, he settled on a common outline which he called the "dramatic structure" (translated from German) which later became known as Freytag's Pyramid, the Plot Pyramid, or the Plot Mountain with five basic elements: Exposition, Rise, Climax, Fall, and Resolution (or Catastrophe in the case of a tragedy). These five have been expanded and further amplified over time to include additional remarks and events along the way, but the basic structure remains intact and used throughout the world by authors, journalists, playwrights, and screenwriters.

In crafting this module to make it more comprehensive and practical to non-professional writers, I created a modified version (Figure 11 below) to give a more accurate depiction of how compelling storytelling unfolds. You'll notice the greater length of the falling action, which is far more representative of the real world, whereas fictional stories typically have long rising action and short falling action.

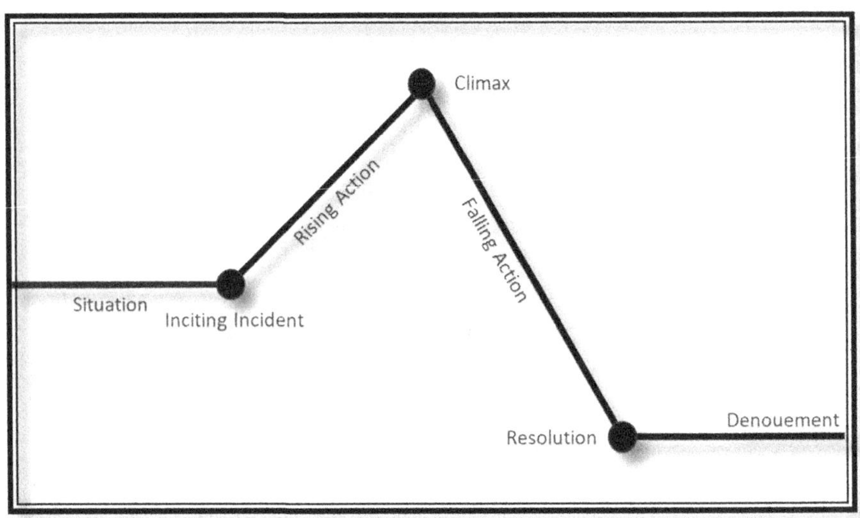

Figure 11 — Modified Freytag's Pyramid

To many of you, this looks familiar from your grammar school days. I have anecdotally surveyed dozens of my class participants over the years from countries around the world, and they near universally remember their homework assignments to read and plot a story's arc from beginning to end. In my own life, I was stunned during a back-to-school night for my then 2nd grade son to see this diagram on the classroom wall.

As a reminder then, here are the subelements of every story.

Situation (a.k.a. Exposition): Description of the basic storyline that exposes the following:

- Protagonist (a.k.a. Champion): The hero whose survival (job, identity, salary) is at stake.
- Antagonist: The person or environment that's trying to thwart the Champion.
- Speaker: The person who's telling the story (may or may not be the Champion).
- Major Characters: Individuals we care about (in a LEFT & SPIE sense).
- Minor Characters: Essential roles, but not usually worth profiling.

- Conflict: The undesirable situation that's been tolerated until now.

Inciting Circumstance: The "thing" that starts the action (e.g., budget approval).

Rising Action: The series of events that happen to (or because of) the main characters.

Complication: An unexpected event that must be overcome before reaching the Climax.

Climax: The turning point where the resolution to the Conflict seems achievable.

Falling Action: Cleaning up all the loose ends.

Resolution: The Conflict has finally been resolved to the Champion's satisfaction.

Denouement: French for "untie the knot," resolving the Conflict creates new opportunities.

Now let's apply this to *The Princess Bride.* Before I give you my answers, test yourself. Take a blank piece of paper and copy Table 14. Then try to fill it in **without** looking at the next page.

Table 14 — Storyline Mapping Template

Situation	
Champion	
Speaker	
Adversary	
Conflict	
Inciting Circumstance	
Rising Action	
Complications	
Climax	
Falling Action	
Resolution	
Denouement	

Table 15 is my take on the plotline. It's okay if you have something different or disagree.

Table 15 — Mapping The Princess Bride

Situation	Friends Westley and Buttercup grew up together, fell in love, and separated by choice. Rumor of Westley's death drives Buttercup into a mood of despair.
Champion	Westley, an intelligent, athletic, swordsman
Speaker	A Grandfather
Adversary	Prince Humperdinck, who wants to marry Buttercup and kill Westley
Conflict	The two lovers have been separated for a long time. Up until now, it's a bearable problem.
Inciting Circumstance	Buttercup is kidnapped by Vizzini, an unbearable situation.
Rising Action	Westley's pursuit of Buttercup to free her from the evil Prince's grasp.
Complications	Sword fight atop the cliffs, rock fight with the giant, battle of wits with Vizzini, ROAS, death, raiding the castle.
Climax	Westley and Buttercup reunite in the castle.
Falling Action	Westley disables the Prince; Inigo Montoya kills the six-fingered man; Fezzik locates horses to make their escape.
Resolution	They all regroup and make their escape from the castle.
Denouement	They ride off into the sunset with the hope of living happily ever after in a castle of their own, with their average 1.9 children (2023 stat) and a white picket moat.

Arriving at these same answers is not the point. Rather, the objective is for you to practice noticing plotlines. The more practice you have with artistic examples (films, books, television shows, etc.) where the consequences of failure are minimal, the better you will be able to apply this technique to real-world presentations. The truth is that just about every real-life story follows this same trajectory.

Table 16 is how I mapped out the eulogy for Doc.

Table 16 - The Eulogy Story

Situation	Shuttle Columbia disintegrates during reentry to landing.
Champion	Dave Brown
Speaker	Jeff Goldfinger
Conflict	Properly honoring Dave's life in the face of international attention.
Initiating Circumstance	Family selects Goldy and Gordon to give eulogies
Rising Action	Designing the eulogy's plotline, deconflicting content with Gordon, gathering specific anecdotes, rehearsing the speech, coordinating travel.
Complications	Weather impact in Houston delaying Shadow Box assembly
Climax	Delivering the Eulogy
Falling Action	Burial and reception
Resolution	Family and friends are in moods of acceptance and serenity
Denouement	A more complete identity of Dave is now known to all

Notice that the first part of the Rising Action, "Designing the Eulogy's Plotline" is itself its own Freytag's Pyramid. This is a truism of life. Every story has stories nested inside. Table 17 articulates the plotline that I started developing just after I received the request to speak at the funeral.

Table 17 — The Story within the Story

Situation	Dave and I had met eighteen years earlier in the Navy. Shared duty stations three times, housemates twice.
Conflict	Dave was never satisfied with the status quo; always trying to better himself.
Initiating Circumstance	Dave becoming a flight surgeon.
Rising Action	His accomplishments along the way from civilian doctor to Navy flight surgeon to pilot to STS-107 Mission Specialist.
Climax	He died doing what he loved the most.
Falling Action	Reminders of all the lives he touched along the way.
Resolution	Dave would want us to move on quickly.
Denouement	A very special renaissance man.

As long as you're watching TV you might as well be productive. Practice plotting the show's (or even a commercial's) storyline using the template in Table 12.

MOODS Я US

System 1's primary driver is emotion. Our emotional responses occur in the limbic area of our brain which evolved with our mammalian ancestors. In that respect, we can view emotion and the physiological states it affects—like heart rate, blood pressure, sensory enhancement, and immune response—as somewhat universally common to all mammals. You, me, a chimp, and a wildebeest would likely share an identical fear response if surprised by a lion.

Mood, by contrast, is largely a human phenomenon that is produced in language with others—a System 2 function. You can imagine our cave dwelling ancestors exchanging the following words:

Barney: *Hey, Fred. Whattya doin'?*

Fred: *Now that Pebbles is off to college, I decided to turn her old cave into a side hustle. Maybe make some money off my rock collection.*

Barney: *You're in a very ambitious mood lately.*

Flores (2012) has a more philosophical interpretation of mood.

> Most people have an interpretation of mood and emotion that limits their power to observe and change their moods ... In speaking of moods, we're not using the word strictly in its usual sense of 'feelings' or 'emotions.' We refer instead to the ways in which people's past experiences predispose them to certain actions."[59]

In other words, think of mood as a foreshadowing of what is likely to happen soon based on a grounded (or not) assessment of the past.

For example, as I started writing this, the world had just emerged from the COVID-19 pandemic. Many countries were in a mood of resolution as they returned to normal, while others were in a mood of despair as new variants drove up hospitalization rates. The travel industry was in a mood of optimism as bookings rose, while the energy sector was in a mood of confusion as the battle between oil and gas versus renewable energy seemed chaotic. Many employees found themselves in a mood of resistance regarding return to office edicts, while others were in a mood of ambition recognizing

59 Flores and Flores, *Conversations for Action and Collected Essays,* 61.

the new opportunities that had emerged because of low unemployment and wage inflation.

Many moods have only appeared in recent history because of our increasingly advanced societies. You would be hard-pressed to imagine a serf living in 8th century medieval Europe being in moods of ambition or optimism about their offspring going off to college. Imagine the moods of Incan, Mayan, Aboriginal Australians, and other Indigenous peoples as boats with strange-looking humans from far off lands suddenly appeared on their shores. With no prior experience of such creatures nor any knowledge of their motives, I suspect that a mood of serenity was not their first reaction.

What's important to understand as a presenter is that your listeners are always in a mood, perhaps multiple moods, simultaneously. As I write this, I am in a mood of ambition about completing this future bestseller, a mood of anxiety for an upcoming trip that includes travel to three continents, a mood of overwhelm as I approach dealing with filing taxes in two countries, and a mood of optimism as the depressed stock market has created tremendous buy-and-hold opportunities.

Assessing Moods

The key then to Telling it Like a Topgun is to assess the moods of your listeners so you can take appropriate action.

Our first activity is to accept that moods come in two basic flavors: restrictive or receptive. As the names imply, restrictive moods prevent us from achieving our objectives while receptive moods increase the probability of a successful outcome. Table 18 below is adapted from Flores' work on the topic.[60] As you read through the lists, notice which moods you resonate with.

Flores and Flores, *Conversations for Action and Collected Essays,* 63-65.

Table 18 — Restrictive Moods that Hold us Back

Restrictive Moods	How It Shows Up in Language (out loud or internal voice)
Arrogance	"I already know what you're presenting. Your interpretation is wrong. You should listen to what I have to say about it instead."
Confusion	"I can't make sense of what you're presenting. I don't know what to do next. I can't listen to this anymore."
Despair	"It doesn't matter what you say, I know that disaster lies ahead, and nothing can be done about it. I give up."
Distrust	"I hear what you're saying but I don't believe that you have my interests at heart."
Panic	"I'm so overwhelmed right now. I can't make any decision so my only option is to work as hard and fast as I can."
Resentment	"It's all their fault and they don't care about us regular people."
Resignation	"This situation will never get better. There's nothing I can do to change it."

RECEPTIVE MOODS THAT MOVE US FORWARD

By contrast, Table 19 highlights some receptive moods we want our listener(s) to embrace.

Table 19 — Receptive Moods that Move Us Forward

Receptive Moods	How It Shows Up in Language
Acceptance	"I understand that there are certain things that are beyond my control, yet I'm grateful for the opportunity to be here and contribute in other ways."

Receptive Moods	How It Shows Up in Language
Ambition	"I see opportunities for me to succeed and I am committed to taking the necessary actions."
Confidence	"I have succeeded at something like this in the past and I'm ready to act effectively now."
Resolution	"I know precisely what immediate action I need to take."
Serenity	"I accept that bad things happen to good people for unexplainable reasons, and I am grateful to be alive."
Trust	"I have an assessment that you care for my concerns and are capable of fulfilling on the commitments you have made to me."
Wonder	"I am unfamiliar with this situation, yet the world seems full of new opportunities and I like it."

Did you notice how your own mood shifted as you were reading through the lists? Did you find yourself recognizing specific moods you regularly experience? Or perhaps you know a few people in your professional or personal life that exhibit one or more of these moods? Notice how quickly you might have shifted from one mood to another.

I enjoyed in the original *Top Gun* how well the students' moods were portrayed. When Kelly McGillis' character Charley is giving a talk to the students, they're all slouching in their seats in a mood of arrogance—Maverick most egregiously, as he relates the story of flying upside down on top of the MiG. (See for yourself: https://youtu.be/wUZxSf_P2r0).

Or consider the mood of confusion and panic on the faces of "Bob" and "Phoenix" in the sequel when the 3-star admiral gives them their new mission parameters that mandate a higher altitude ingress at a slower speed and extended time. As Maverick enters the training range and declares a Time-on-Target (TOT) of 2:15, "Payback"s mood shifts to skepticism as he says: "That's impossible." Finally, with 16 hundredths of a second left on the countdown time Maverick's bombs hit the bullseye while he's pulling 10g's in the jet (the most I ever experienced was 8 so he's got me there), the mood once again shifts to something more receptive such as ambition and resolution and they all realize it *can* be done his way. (See: https://youtu.be/DqRxGuBSvlU).

Your mission for every presentation is to engineer the most receptive moods. As you design your slide deck, consider what moods you might provoke along the way and how you might ethically manipulate an appropriate mood shift. For example, if you're briefing a risky project idea (like I often do) to someone who is risk averse (like my wife), you're likely to trigger a restrictive mood (ah, the summation of my marriage). Conversely, that same idea pitched to a risk seeker is likely to trigger moods of ambition and resolution.

We don't have moods. Moods have us.

- Fernando Flores

Our emotions react almost instantly to sensory inputs. Our ancestors' System 1 brain processed the lion's movement in the grass from their peripheral vision, which triggered several immediate physiological reactions that shifted their gaze, increased their heart rate, shut down digestion, increased blood flow and tightened muscles. Like emotions, our System 2 moods quickly appear as a reaction to a new situation we find ourselves in. See the blue plus sign in the pregnancy test and *voilà*, not only will you have a physiological response (most likely a heart rate increase) but also moods of wonder, ambition, and resolution if this was part of your plan … or perhaps anxiety, despair, and panic if you were 52 at the time, already had two adult daughters from your first marriage, and just found out that your 40-year-old second wife was pregnant even though when you first met you agreed that neither of you wanted to have kids.

Yep, that's what really happened to me. However, as my System 2 kicked in, I soon shifted my mood to joy and anticipation for the new possibilities of being a different dad the second time around. I was more emotionally and financially secure and no longer in the Navy, having to miss critical events because I was halfway around the world in the middle of an ocean.

The other difference between System 1 emotions and System 2 moods is the fleeting nature of emotions. Remove the stimulus (like the lion chasing us) and the physiological response returns to normal. That's the job of our croc brain deep inside System 1. The automatic systems are designed to keep us in homeostasis—the technical term for normal heart rate, breathing, temperature, digestion, etc.

System 2 moods can be more pervasive and also contagious. Hearing your child's fetal heartbeat or seeing the ultrasound for the first time produces a certain contagious mood for both parents that can last for hours or days. That pregnant glow can "infect" friends and coworkers.

Restrictive moods are also contagious. We've all worked with at least one Eeyore-type that tries to sprinkle their woe-is-me despair on everyone else in the office.

Now that we know moods are reactions to situations and that they can be contagious, there's another aspect we need to be aware of not only when designing our presentation but also during the delivery. As described in Table 20 below, moods exist in a broad spectrum of time domains.

TABLE 20 — MOODS ARE TEMPORAL

Time Domain	Description	How it appears in language
Reactive	Personally experienced by a momentary event	"Crap, I just got fired." "I just finished my PMP certification. Now I can apply for that other job."
Situational	Moods that appear in a group setting requiring cooperation.	"We just got word that the merger has been approved. We all need to prepare for some changes to our processes." "We were just assigned a new project. I wonder how this group will be able to execute it by the deadline."

Time Domain	Description	How it appears in language
Prevailing	Moods that have a long-term duration caused by external events at scale	"I'm resigned to working from home while the pandemic is still affecting our area." "This recession has lasted much longer than any economist predicted."
Epochal	Moods that affect us over sustained periods lasting decades or more	"I'm really confused by the digital age. I'm worried that I've given up too much privacy in exchange for convenience." "Government budgets and corporate pensions are going to be under severe strain in the coming decades as the world's population is rapidly aging and birth rates are declining. I don't know how we're going to cope as a nation."

Make a table of the four temporal domains of moods and make some notes about how your audience might be gripped. For example, as I'm writing this in March 2024, AI seems to have become both a Situational and Prevailing mood, depending on what industry you might be in.

THEY TRUST THEIR EARS

"If people like you they'll listen to you, but if they trust you they'll do business with you."

- Zig Zigler, Public Speaker and Entrepreneur

Professor Paul Zak is a drug pusher. Not in a Walter White "Breaking Bad" kinda way. Rather, he has spent most of his career studying the effects of oxytocin on human behavior. Zak analyzed oxytocin levels in blood samples. Sometimes he dosed his subjects using an oxytocin-infused nasal spray. Other times he just used video clips that tugged at your heartstrings (think Budweiser's Clydesdales ads) compared against more bland content (think Bob "The Happy Painter" Ross). His results show that oxytocin is largely responsible for what allows humans to trust one another.[61] Zak and his coauthors found they could artificially increase, by a whopping 47%, the dollar amount of a charitable donation by dosing their subjects with this specific neurotransmitter.[62] So there you have it: Zak is to blame for all those Sarah McLachlan dog adoption commercials.

As I mentioned earlier, we modern humans are outstanding at making stuff up. What allowed us to survive and thrive as we evolved in a dangerous world was having collective beliefs in particular fictional tales that were used to organize large groups, such as:

- "As your Pharaoh, you can trust that I'll protect you from invaders."
- "Trust me, this small round piece of metal with the king's picture on one side is worth two loaves of bread."
- "We hold these truths to be self-evident…" (Opening phrase from the US Declaration of Independence)

For all your presentations, no matter which of the four scenarios you are designing towards, you must address the following two questions:

Why should your listener(s) trust you and/or your organization?

How can you produce an assessment of trustworthiness?

Option 1) Spike the drinking water with oxytocin.

Option 2) Put canisters of oxytocin nasal spray in the air conditioning ducts.

61 Paul J. Zak, Robert Kurzban and William T. Matzner, "The neurobiology of trust" in *Annals of the New York Academy of Sciences,* 1032(1), 2004, 224-227.

62 Jorge A. Barraza, Michael E. McCullough, Sheila Ahmadi and Paul J. Zak, "Oxytocin infusion increases charitable donations regardless of monetary resources" in *Hormones and Behavior,* Volume 60, Issue 2, 2011, 148-151.

Obviously, we aren't allowed to perform *chemical* manipulation with our listener(s). Instead, let me try a hypothetical story. I just moved into your neighborhood and come knocking on your door to ask if you can recommend a trustworthy dentist and auto mechanic. You would likely recommend your current providers. If they weren't trustworthy, you wouldn't keep going to them for service. However, if I asked you if you trust your dentist to work on your car, or more absurdly, asked you if I can trust your mechanic to work on my teeth, you would think I blew a fuse in my brain's circuit breaker panel.

As you can see, making an assessment of trustworthiness is a bit more nuanced than the actions of a single neurotransmitter. That's why we need to implement a powerful linguistic interpretation to win their hearts and minds. Flores[63] claims that we decide who to trust (or not) based on our assessments of four observable attributes (using the mnemonic EARS):

Engagement: A commitment to take care of a customer's present and future concerns

Ability: Competence to perform the task

Reliability: Ability to manage one's commitments

Sincerity: When spoken words match one's inner voice

When I was living in San Diego, California, I took my car to New Way Auto Services, and I took my teeth to Scripps Rock Dental. If anyone moved to town near us and asked me if I could recommend a trustworthy dentist and auto mechanic, I never hesitated to recommend either one. Here's why:

E FOR ENGAGEMENT

Walking into their facilities for the first time, it was obvious they were engaged in their chosen fields. New Way Auto had multiple bays with electric lifts for the cars, pressure washers, and drills. Scripps Rock Dental had multiple chairs with electric recline for my body, pressure washers, and electric drills. If the mechanic had been working out of the garage at his house, I'd have been more than a bit skeptical about his ability to take care of my car's needs on an ongoing basis. Similarly, if the dentist rented a

63 Flores and Flores, *Conversations for Action and Collected Essays*, 69-74.

mobile office trailer with a placard that read Teeth Я Us stuck on the side, I'd doubt his ability to handle a root canal procedure. Other indications I observed were business licenses and professional certificates on the walls, organized and clean waiting rooms, systems to organize appointments, and an ability to accept payments—all indications of a thriving and engaged small business.

Make a list of things that can prove your engagement with your topic such as: your monetary investment, your facility, the time you've spent on the project, etc.

A FOR ABILITY

Engagement by itself is an insufficient metric to assess trustworthiness. I needed to know, once my car was in the air or my butt was in the chair, that they could perform the work competently. Here's where you must stand back and ask yourself a simple question: Am I competent to judge the competence of others?

As a teen, I owned a 1971 Dodge Charger with an 8-cylinder, 383 cubic inch engine and 4-barrel Holly carburetor—a classic muscle car. Although I did a lot of my own repairs, including a complete carb rebuild, that clearly doesn't put me on par with Mona Lisa Vito (shout out to Marisa Tomei's Oscar winning performance in *My Cousin Vinny*). Even more absurd, I was (and still am) completely incompetent to assess my dentist's ability to rebuild my teeth.

In this case, I had to trust in the competence of others' ability to assess their ability. I know that sounds like a circular argument, but this is why we have licensing and certification organizations. In the case of New Way Auto, I observed certificates on the wall indicating all their mechanics had been certified by the National Institute for Automotive Service Excellence (ASE), the industry standard. At Scripps Rock Dental, each of the two dentists had their dental school Doctor of Dental Surgery (DDS) diplomas on the wall along with their Board certifications.

This is where *TOPGUN*'s "Best of the Best" notion comes from. If you're going to stand in front of a room full of your peers explaining how they should and shouldn't fly in combat, they must know that you are absolutely able to do the same.

This is a good time for a short sightseeing flight. Hang with me while we take a detour.

In the late 1970s, the Air Force observed that despite all pilots receiving the exact same initial training, years later there was a large difference between each pilots' skills. The US Air Force Office of Scientific Research hired sibling Professors Stuart and Hubert Dreyfus, from the University of California, Berkeley, to study how pilots acquire and hone their skills over time. The outcome of the Dreyfus brothers' research, published in 1980, resulted in what is now popularly known as the Dreyfus Model of Skill Acquisition[64].

Their original 5-stage model has since been updated to include a 6th stage as articulated in Table 21:

Table 21 — Dreyfus' Model of Skill Acquisition

Stage	Main Action Characteristic
Novice	Explicitly follows the rules
Advanced Beginner	Recognizes that rules can be conditional
Competent	Can prioritize the rules in complex scenarios
Proficient	Actions move from System 2 → 1 as "muscle memory" and intuition appear
Expert	"Rules? I don't need no stinkin' rules." Can react to rapidly changing conditions
Master	Creates new rules for the community

64 S.E. Dreyfus and Hubert L. Dreyfus, *A five-stage model of the mental activities involved in directed skill acquisition* (University of California, Berkeley, 1980).

On this scale, I'd be a novice (e.g., incompetent) at dentistry, an advanced beginner at auto repair, competent at cooking, proficient at playing piano, an expert in proposal writing, and humbly, a master public speaker.

My mechanic and dentist have passed the first two tests – engagement and ability. By themselves, the two attributes are essential but still insufficient.

What makes you able to do this? List any certifications, degrees, prior accomplishments, etc. that you could insert into your speech.

R FOR RELIABILITY

I really appreciated the ability of both these providers to live up to their scheduling commitments. If the mechanic said the car would be ready by the end of the day, it was. And if there was going to be a delay, he would immediately call me and explain the reason (e.g., had to special order a part). Same held true at my dentist's office. If the provider isn't reliable, they aren't trustworthy.

Caveat: You may decide that these three attributes aren't evenly weighted. For example, if I am diagnosed with a brain tumor, then I'll want to be treated by a surgeon with master level skills. If my appointment is at 9:00 a.m., I'll be happy to wait an entire day just to see her. A yearly physical exam is not the same situation.

As before, while these three attributes are also essential, they're still insufficient. There's one more, crucial attribute that stands out among the bunch.

As with the first two attributes, list one or more that describe how reliable you (your company or product) are.

S FOR SINCERITY

Hands down, what I most appreciated about New Way Auto was the manager's sincerity. I specifically remember when my daughter visited me from Nevada with her old beater car. She was just a few weeks away from selling it and moving to New Zealand to attend college. I felt and heard some sounds from the undercarriage that made me think failing wheel bearings or something equally troublesome (being the advanced beginner mechanic that I am).

So, I took it to New Way Auto. Sure enough, there was something significant wrong but after I shared my daughter's situation, he said it wasn't worth trying to fix it. Her investment in the fix wouldn't be re-couped by a higher sale price just a few weeks away and it was safe enough to drive in the meantime. When the time came to sell it, my daughter sincerely shared this finding with the buyer.

Of the four attributes, sincerity is the most difficult to observe. By definition, the adjective means "honesty of mind; freedom from hypocrisy."[65] Well, how do we know the honesty of someone else's mind? The practical interpretation I use goes something like this: if their words go against their own self-interest, that's a good measure of sincerity. For example, New Way Auto went counter to their own financial interest when recommending my daughter not have her car fixed. When Dr. Hatch would examine my teeth, he would always end our sessions with, "I wish you would brush your teeth and floss more." This was counter to his interest because by not brushing or flossing, there would be a higher probability of my need for more "shovel ready" dental work. (It hurts just thinking about it.)

As a corporate trainer and consultant, one of the first things I tell new clients is that my job is to work my way out of a job. In other words, my goal is to teach them the skills they need to succeed without my help—teach them how to swim across the lake on their own.

When I moved to Broadlands, Virginia, I had to find a new auto mechanic. The "easy button" was right across the street called Honest-1 Auto Care®, a franchise of the nationwide chain. Notice the name. It says something right away about the perceived dishonesty of the auto repair industry. How could I know if it would live up to its name? Today we have an easy way to read all the gossip about a product or service provider—

65 https://www.merriam-webster.com/dictionary/sincerity

online reviews. With a 4.9 rating averaged over hundreds of reviews, I felt confident I could trust Honest-1.

If my first test of sincerity is to listen for words and look for actions that go against the individual or company's financial interests, my second test is the corollary. If their advice supports their best interest, at least they should say so. For example, at the beginning of this book, I clearly pointed out that I am not a TOPGUN instructor and that I used this title purposefully to take advantage of the pop culture phenomenon. Had I published this book years ago, or many years from now, it would most likely have a different title. But at least I'm sincere.

The French company Ipsos did a survey titled "Veracity Index 2022" (Figure 12). I'm gratified to see that the STEM educated are in the top five. Notice auto mechanics are in the bottom half and "politicians generally" are dead last. Why is that? I have a grounded assessment that relates to politicians' abject hypocrisy. When something is in their best interest (votes) they tell you it's in yours. Many of them (on both sides of the political spectrum) vociferously declare that they're fighting for the interests of the "common man" (or woman, or course) when they're really fighting for the benefit of their biggest campaign donors. As I said, this is a grounded assessment backed up by independently verifiable assertions of fact from all over the world, in every system, from democratic to autocratic.

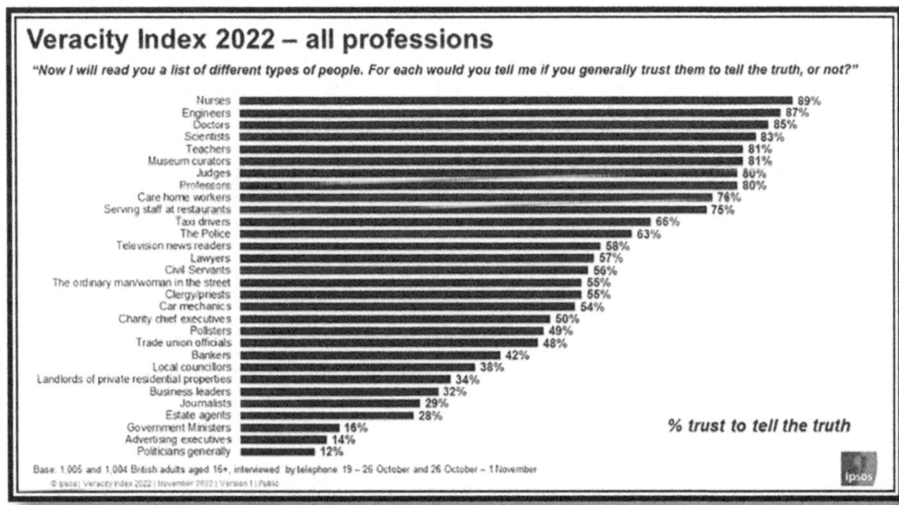

Figure 12 - Who do you trust?[66]

66 https://www.ipsos.com/en-uk/ipsos-veracity-index-2022

"Trust but verify."

~ President Ronald Reagan

In God we trust. All others we monitor.

~ motto of the US Naval Intelligence Corps

In closing out this section, the most important thing to remember about trust can be stated thusly:

Trust shouldn't be viewed as a permanent character trait but rather as a grounded, domain-specific, assessment of someone's or something's ability to fulfill a promise.

If we're too trusting (naïve), we might be taken advantage of. If we're too skeptical, then we might miss incredible opportunities. Prudence is the operative word.

Go through your list of trustworthy attributes and select at least one from each category appropriate to your audience to include in the design of your presentation.

MAKE IT COMPELLING CHECKLIST

MAKE IT COMPELLING

1. Your customer's story .... PLOT THEIR PYRAMID

NOTE

There are two stories in every presentation: the story your listener has and your story. Use the blank form provided earlier to first diagnose your listener's story. If it is a company, search their website for clues: About page, Press Releases, regulatory filings, etc. If it is an individual, use the same profiling TTPs mentioned earlier, but now from the perspective of the story they're living in.

2. Structure your presentation .... PLOT YOUR PYRAMID
3. Listener's existing moods .... RECEPTIVE OR RESISTIVE
4. If resistive .... DESIGN RECEPTIVE
5. Trust .... PROVE IT
    a. Engaged
    b. Able
    c. Reliable
    d. Sincere
6. Speech Acts .... CHECK
    a. ASSERTIONS are true and sincere
    b. ASSESSMENTS are grounded by factual assertions
    c. DECLARATIONS are fully described

STEP 5: MAKE IT VISUAL

I shall not today attempt further to define the kinds of material I understand to be embraced within that shorthand description, and perhaps I could never succeed in intelligibly doing so. But I know it when I see it, and the motion picture involved in this case is not that.

~ US Supreme Court Justice Potter Stewart

QED: I'LL KNOW IT WHEN I SEE IT

In the Spring of 1948, just three years after World War II, some of the world's most renowned theoreticians gathered at a hotel in the Pocono mountains of Pennsylvania to reconnect to their passion for physics. The conference was convened by the National Academy of Sciences to discuss, among other topics in quantum mechanics, the vexing nature of quantum electrodynamics (QED).

Don't worry if you don't understand anything about QED. Neither do I, so I made it irrelevant to the story.

In attendance were two very intelligent young men around thirty years old. One had a hand in the development of radar during the war. The other worked on the design of the first atom bombs. They were each scheduled to give oral presentations to an audience that included both present and future Nobel laureates. As one biographer frames the situation, "[their] first big conference with big men."[67] This was akin to a TOPGUN murder board on steroids.

At the time, physics was all about phormulas … I mean formulas (sheesh, the English language is weird).

The first speaker, Julian Schwinger, the radar man (if he was a fellow flyboy in the Navy, we would've nicknamed him "Tron"), was a proponent

---

67 Jagdish Metra, *The Beat of a Different Drum: The life and science of Richard Feynman.* (Clarendon Press, 1994), 217.

of such formulas to describe his notion of quantum field theory. Following Schwinger was Richard Feynman, known for bombarding (pun intended) theoretical physics with common sense. He had always been considered more of an intuitive thinker and, in his desire to understand the QED theory, he designed a "wiring diagram" to graphically illustrate what was happening to the subatomic particles (Figure 13). Known as Feynman Diagrams, even Schwinger, who often disagreed with Feynman, saw the value of such a compelling visual explanation "... the Feynman diagram was bringing computation to the masses."[68]

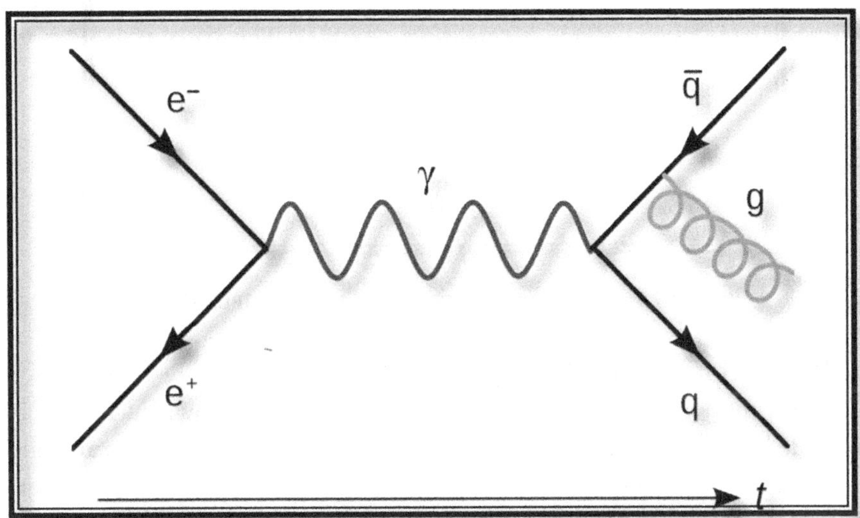

FIGURE 13 — FEYNMAN'S GRAPHICAL REPRESENTATION OF HIS QED THEORY

Feynman understood the power of "seeing is believing" and went on to be awarded a Nobel Prize in physics for his work on QED and his diagrams are now universally taught in higher education physics curricula.

---

68 J. Schwinger, "Quantum Electrodynamics – An Individual View" in *Journal de Physique Colloques, 43* (C8), 1982, 416.

OUR EYES DON'T SEE A THING

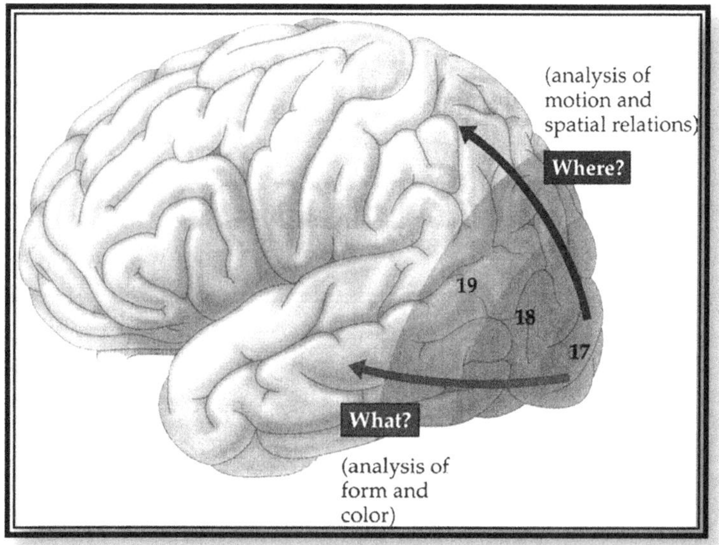

Figure 14 - Seeing is Believing ... in Multiple Places

We're primarily visual beings. By some accounts more than 50% of our brain matter is devoted to visual processing.[69] As shown in Figure 14, multiple lobes and discrete areas within each lobe parse the image and then assemble the parts looking for a match. We have one area that just processes horizontal lines and two others for vertical and diagonal, respectively. Yet another area, the fusiform gyrus, is dedicated solely to facial recognition.

As discussed earlier, cave paintings by our ancestors emerged about 50,000 years ago with handprints—the OG of selfies. According to one recent paper in the journal Nature, we've been telling stories via cave paintings as early as 44,000 years ago[70]. Yet it took another 40,000 years for the first alphabet to emerge[71]. In other words, graphic artists as influencers have been around an order of magnitude longer than the first papyrus bloggers. Tweet that!

---

69 Concepts and Figure 14 illustration from S. Hagen, "The mind's eye" in *Rochester Review,* 74(4), 2012, 32 – 37.

70 M. Aubert et al., "Earliest hunting scene in prehistoric art" in *Nature,* 576(7787), 2019, 442-445.

71 B.S. Isserlin and J. Boardman, "The earliest alphabetic writing" in *The Cambridge ancient history, 3*(Part 1) 1982.

It took another thousand years for math to manifest so that ancient Babylonians could properly calculate and collect taxes. And probably only a month later for a law firm to locate the first offshore tax haven.

I point to these facts as a reminder that interpreting words and numbers doesn't come naturally. We must be taught these skills which are computationally expensive in our brains. Think image analysis as a System 1 function while System 2 takes care of reading, writing, and arithmetic-ing.

Here are other basic facts about our visual systems that can be useful considerations in the design of your presentations:

- Rods and cones' primary purpose is about peripheral motion and central focus; secondarily about black and white versus color vision.
- It takes thousands of times longer (up to 60,000 times by some accounts) to process a word than it does to process an image.
- The brain will always fill in missing visual pieces, which explains why we're susceptible to optical illusions.
- Fonts can be fatiguing. Thousands of studies have examined the difference between serif and sans serif typefaces—sans wins the speed race.
- Fonts of unusual **size, SHAPE,** or contrast will attract the viewer's deeper attention—disfluency wins the memory race[72].
- Chromostereopsis, overlapping colors at opposite ends of the spectrum (e.g., red text on blue background or vice versa), is extremely fatiguing as the lens tries to simultaneously focus both wavelengths.

I could write an entire book on how to design slides but I'm neither a graphic artist nor do I play one on TV. My default position for high consequence presentations is to engage a professional if time and money permit. When I served at all three weapons schools, we had a dedicated graphic arts department with a specific artist permanently assigned to each lecturer for consistency. In my post-Navy corporate employee and

72 C. Diemand-Yauman, D.M. and E.B. Vaughan, E. B. Fortune favors the bold *(and the italicized)*: Effects of disfluency on educational outcomes. *Cognition, 118*(1), 2011, 111-115.

consulting work, I've noticed that even startup companies have artists on staff or independent contractors that can be hired by the hour or project.

Having recommended outsourcing your slide deck graphics, it is both useful and necessary to have some basic understanding of industry TTPs so that you can provide proper guidance to and oversight of your artist. The next two sections summarize the accumulation of my four decades of presenting interspersed with the brain science to back it up.

A PICTURE IS WORTH 1,000 WORDS

Statistician and political scientist Edward Tufte has made it his life's work to help engineers and scientists visualize their data in ways that convey meaning. One of the examples he cites is Charles Minard's depiction of Napoleon's march to Moscow (Figure 15), "...[p]robably the best statistical graphic ever drawn."[73]

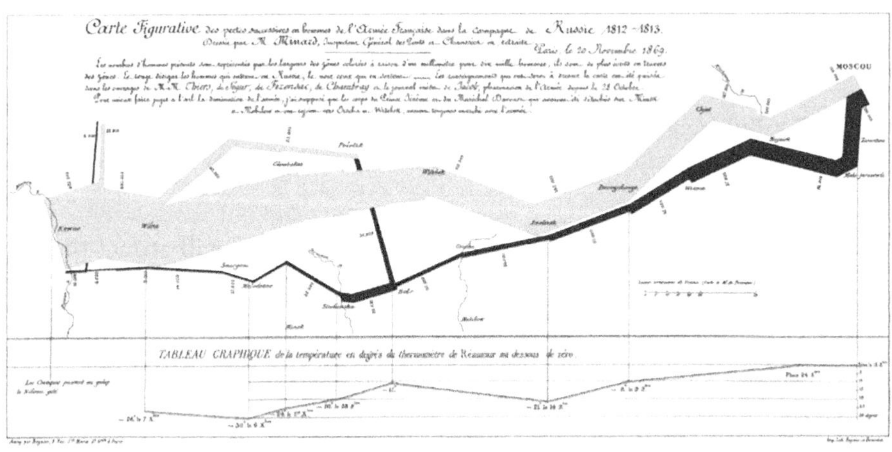

FIGURE 15 — NAPOLEON'S MARCH
AS ILLUSTRATED BY FRENCH CIVIL ENGINEER CHARLES MINARD, 1869

If a picture is worth a thousand words, how should we decide which pictures to use in our presentations?

For those of you old enough to remember the 80s, besides Queen's "Note Heard Around the World" at Live Aid, terrestrial tussles between Star

73 E.R. Tufte and P.R. Graves-Morris, (1983). *The visual display of quantitative information,* Vol. 2, No. 9. (Cheshire, CT: Graphics press, 1983).

Wars and Star Trek, the chilling end of the Cold War, and Joe Montana's gridiron greatness with the 49ers, digital speedometers were all the rage. Almost overnight, LCD and LED technology became cheap and reliable enough to replace analog mechanical devices. There was only one problem. It turned out to decrease safety.

Because our brains are pattern-making machines, our ability to recognize the position of the speedometer's needle as being left or right of normal is rather trivial. To decode a sequence of horizontal and vertical lines, convert them to numbers, then calculate whether the numbers are above or below a specifically recalled threshold requires far more processing time. So, while digital displays became ubiquitous in cars by the 1990s, manufacturers switched to a digital representation of an analog speedometer, until the Toyota Prius and Teslas emerged on the market.

Not all digital is bad. It needs to be applied where the computational cost is appropriate.

- Analog speedometer good. Digital bad.
- Analog radio dial bad. Digital good.

In other words, it's not that digital is better or worse than analog. As with everything in life, context counts.

One of the rare cases of a well-designed government document, the US Transportation Security Agency (TSA) uses a variety of graphical means to send a compelling message about firearms being detected at airport checkpoints (see Figure 16). I didn't choose this infographic to have a debate about gun safety. Rather, I ask that whichever side of the argument you're on, put that aside and just focus on the selection of graphical elements while you notice the following as I walk your eyes around the page clockwise:

FIGURE 16 — TSA'S FIREARMS REPORT (2014 EDITION)

Color Contrast: The largest number on the page (2,212) is placed on a white background to help it stand out.

Letters vs. Numbers: The word six spelled out draws our attention. In a sea of large numbers, spelling out a small number can help highlight a particular data point.

Map vs. Table: Instead of a map, imagine the designer had used a table with the airports listed in the first column and amounts in the second column. The map helps to add a layer of geographical analysis hard to convey in a table.

Circle Size: Using different circle sizes to represent relative amounts immediately draws our attention to the cities with the biggest problem—of course it's Texas, where everything is just … bigger.

Pie Chart: Whenever you have a small number of data points where one is overwhelming the other, the "Pac-Man" style pie chart captures the lopsided ratio of the variables (only two, in this case).

Bar Chart vs. Table: Lastly, the bar chart, like the map, could've been expressed as a two-column table with the years in the first column and amounts in the second. Notice how the bar chart illustrates something of an exponential growth, an analysis nearly impossible to convey in a table without using words to highlight it.

Unethical Manipulation: Regardless of my praise for the bulk of this infographic, I do have a complaint about the bar chart. Notice the size of the first bar: 660. Now look at the last bar: 2,212. The latter is mathematically 3.3 times the size of the first although the bar itself is 8.5 times longer. So, either they (a) gapped the lower half of the chart to save space, or (b) deliberately manipulated the relative size of the bars to force an interpretation of exponential growth. "Just say no" to such TTPs.

They must have heard me talking behind their backs, because I just measured the bar charts for 2019, 2020, and 2021 and the lengths are now proportionate. Shout out to the TSA!

Check out the latest full color version online so you can see what a well done set of graphics looks like.

https://www.tsa.gov/blog/2020/01/15/tsa-year-review-2019

Tufte cautions us to let the data tell the story by picking the most useful representation. In Table 22 below I've provided a summary of the most common methods of displaying various data types along with my own simplified interpretation of the advantages and disadvantages.

TABLE 22 — PROS AND CONS FOR ILLUSTRATING VARIOUS DATA TYPES

Data Type	Primarily Used For	Pros	Cons
Tables	Compliance matrices & demonstrating richness of datasets	Allows for a "clean" look	High brain energy consumption needed to analyze
Charts	Displays relative importance	Easy to interpret	May not convey the entire message
Videos & Photos	Proves the existence of your product/service (factual assertion)	Helps build trust	Can be perceived as gratuitous if not properly explained
Schematics & Blueprints	Demonstrates competency & competitive advantage	Helps built trust & justify value	Requires technical knowledge to interpret
Interim Drawings	Demonstrates progress	Solicits customer feedback and collaboration	Invites criticism
Artist's Conception	Presents fully formed vision	Prevents the reader from creating their own mental image	May need to justify design choices

STOP STARING AT THE MONA LISA

In both the presentation and proposal writing industries, one of the most hotly debated questions that every expert practitioner faces is: What's the right balance of graphics and text?

As US Supreme Court Justice Potter Stewart asserted about his threshold test for obscenity back in 1964: "I know it when I see it."

That's pretty much the same response audience members will have about the balance between graphics and text in your presentation—they'll know it as a gut feeling. However, based on a combination of my own experience, advice I've received from professional graphics artists, and, of course, the latest brain science, here are some TTPs to embrace in your tradeoff:

- Images give the *what;* text gives the *why.*
- Mix up the sequence by putting a word slide after every few graphics and vice versa.
- On word slides, no more than six bullets per slide.
- No text wrapping. Every bullet should be a single line.
- The busier the slide, the lower the viewer's retention.
- Avoid "Louvre titles" (Figure 17)

What's a Louvre title you ask?

This is a pejorative term for treating images like a museum display. Recall any museum you've been to (The Louvre or otherwise) and below the object behind the glass is a simple plaque that reads "The Mona Lisa" or "Tyrannosaurus Rex Jawbone" or "Silver-The Lone Ranger's Horse." This is the corporate equivalent of a slide with your organization chart and the title reads "Org Chart."

No sh*t, Sherlock.

The words in the title should educate the viewer about the key takeaways from the image. Many presenters follow the convention of putting the takeaway at the bottom of the slide in a call out box. That's boring.

Seduce the viewer by capturing their attention right away, at the top of the screen. The title shouldn't answer "what" they're looking at but "why."

FIGURE 17 — (CHOOSE THE BEST TITLE FROM THE LIST BELOW)

So, let's take the Louvre's Mona Lisa as an example of how best to title a slide.

Bad: The Mona Lisa

Good: Mona Lisa can pose for portraits.

Better: Mona Lisa has successfully posed for six portraits.

Best: Mona Lisa is 26.3% more efficient in posing for portraits.

One New Application of CALIPSO - Ocean Windspeed

CIVIL & OPERATIONAL SPACE

- The Cox-Munk Equation relates ocean wind speed to surface reflectivity
- Was applied previously to LITE space-based lidar data by Menzies, Tratt, and Hunt
- Yong has submitted a paper showing global comparison of passive microwave system AMSR-E on Aqua to CALIPSO measured Ocean Windspeed
  - Preliminary results show agreement is better than 1.3 m/s rms using single laser shots
- Trades –
  - Microwave systems give superior all-weather performance
  - CALIPSO measures over much smaller footprint (70 m vs. 20 km)
  - CALIPSO is calibrated using reflectivity from upper atmosphere
- Working towards using ocean surface as an independent lidar calibration and also as independent check on column aerosol extinction.

FIGURE 18 — AN OPPORTUNITY TO IMPROVE THE MESSAGE

Figure 18 is an example from a slide I found online. I have no issue with purely textual slides. In fact, I recommend that after a handful of rich graphics to wake up the brain with 1 - 2 text slides. So it's not about which is better—graphics or text. It's about mixing it up from time-to-time to keep the brain from getting bored.

In the next two figures (19 and 20) I demonstrate how I might have produced a cleaner, more readable version broken up into two slides.

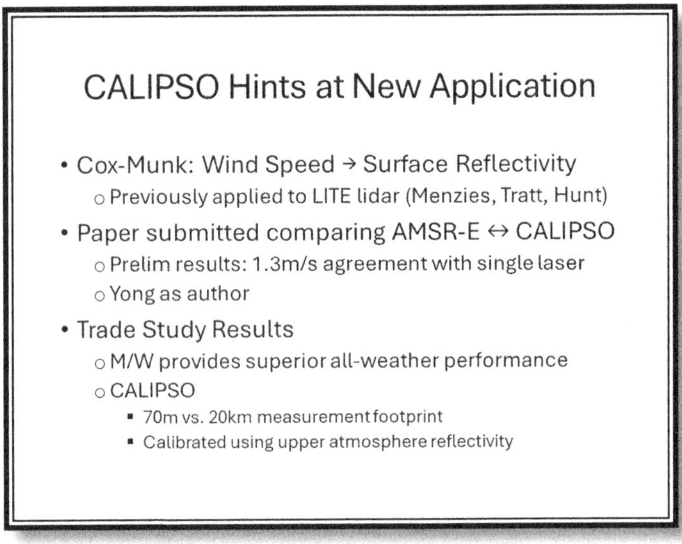

CALIPSO Hints at New Application

- Cox-Munk: Wind Speed → Surface Reflectivity
  - o Previously applied to LITE lidar (Menzies, Tratt, Hunt)
- Paper submitted comparing AMSR-E ↔ CALIPSO
  - o Prelim results: 1.3m/s agreement with single laser
  - o Yong as author
- Trade Study Results
  - o M/W provides superior all-weather performance
  - o CALIPSO
    - ▪ 70m vs. 20km measurement footprint
    - ▪ Calibrated using upper atmosphere reflectivity

FIGURE 19 - CALIPSO DO-OVER #1

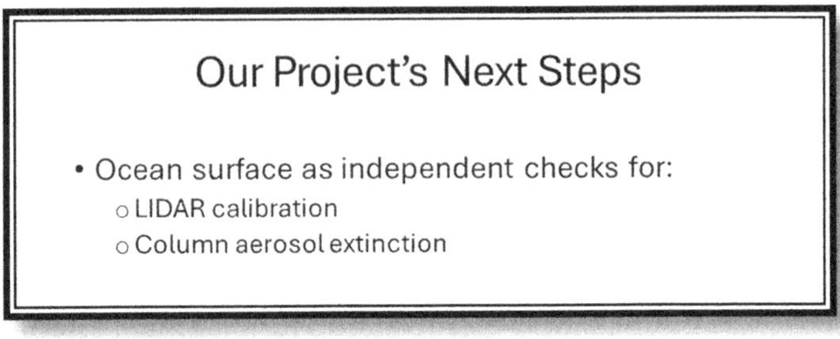

Our Project's Next Steps

- Ocean surface as independent checks for:
  - o LIDAR calibration
  - o Column aerosol extinction

FIGURE 20 - CALIPSO DO-OVER #2

The following are the key takeaways from my review of the slide:

1. Avoid text that wraps around. Keep everything on one line.
2. No need to be grammatically correct.
   a. Eliminate conjunctions, prepositions, and pronouns
   b. Retain nouns, verbs, adverbs, adjectives

Lastly, when first sitting down to design your slide, instead of jumping on the computer, take a moment to pencil out the idea. This is especially helpful when you need to gather information from colleagues. You can use fake data as a place holder.

For example, let's refer to the TSA firearms infographic in Figure 16. Imagine that I was charged with putting together a presentation for my boss to deliver at the annual Governor's conference. I might have gone to my analyst with a hand drawn sheet of paper and said: "Can you get me the accurate data for the placeholder charts I have here?"

Alright, now it's time for you to start designing your slides.

MAKE IT VISUAL CHECKLIST

MAKE IT VISUAL

1. Gather your data .... CHECK

WARNING

When requesting data from other colleagues, you can use fake data to help relay the narrative concept. Be sure to label it as fake. Be sure to review all slides for removal of fake data prior to final rehearsal.

NOTE

In gathering the data you want to present, consider elements that will prove your trustworthiness (Engagement, Ability, Reliability, & Sincerity). Use SPIE to help chose US elements (e.g. using the same testing lab that your customer uses).

2. Images, charts, tables, others .... SELECT MOST APPROPRIATE
3. Slide Titles .... AVOID LOUVRE
4. Font typeface, size, color scheme .... SELECT
5. Sequencing .... VARIABLE

Intersperse graphical and textual slides such that there are no sequences of more than 3 – 4 of either type before switching.

6. Speech Acts .... CHECK
    a. ASSERTIONS are true and sincere
    b. ASSESSMENTS are grounded by factual assertions
    c. DECLARATIONS are fully described

STEP 6: MAKE A REQUEST

I'm gonna make him an offer he can't refuse.

~ Don Vito Corleone, *The Godfather*

A ROAD TO ACTION: PART II

As mentioned earlier, there are a total of five Speech Acts that are part of every oral presentation. Earlier in the book I covered the first three: Assertions, Assessments, and Declarations. As we wind down the design phase, there are two more to round out our list: Offers and Requests. This is where the mnemonic ***A ROAD to Action*** came from:

A for Assertions

R for Requests

O for Offers

A for Assessments

D for Declarations

OFFERS

In business, your offer is simply the product or service you're selling (recall that "selling" doesn't necessarily involve an exchange of currency). This book is my offer to help you design and deliver your oral presentations. Fast-food restaurants offer food served quickly at a low price. Engineers offer elegant design solutions. Accountants offer tax strategies and filing services.

From a philosophical perspective, an offer is when you can help someone (or an organization) take care of their survival needs, however they define survival. For some, it is to spend the least amount of money possible. For others it is to make sure the product lasts as long as possible. Making offers of help to each other in our tribes is what allowed our ancestors to survive, thrive, and grow our communities. Those that refused to help or didn't have the wherewithal were eventually sent away from the tribe to fend for themselves.

There are two relevant distinctions to note regarding making offers to your listeners. First, nobody in your audience should be judging the validity of your offer. A fast-food restaurant's offer is just as valid as the upscale steak house. They both earn money for their owners/franchisees. They both serve their customers' needs for calories. They both support their local economies by hiring staff. The quality of the offer is always in the eye of the customer.

Second, your offer must be congruent with your customer's/listener's needs. For example, you wouldn't see a steak house making offers (e.g.,, advertising) during the Saturday morning cartoon hours on TV, nor are you likely to find a fast-food restaurant advertising during the Sunday morning political talk shows.

For Doc's eulogy, I didn't make an offer. Instead, I made a request, the fifth and final speech act.

REQUESTS

Requests for help are the flip side of the offers coin. Offers are never accepted unless there's an explicit or implicit request to fulfill a need. The restaurant is only making offers because we humans have requested to be fed.

While this book is an overt offer, the impetus for it came from a customer request. In the introduction, I explained that one of my corporate clients asked if I could develop and deliver a public speaking course—a Request.

The order in which the two speech acts—Offers and Requests—occur is not important. Sometimes you'll make an offer to your listener before they make a request. Other times they'll make a request which leads to your offer. In either case, for a transaction to occur both sides must cooperate to fulfill each other's needs.

You might assume that customers (listeners) only make requests and suppliers (presenters) only make offers. The truth is that the two speech acts are as intimately connected as fraternal twins. Whenever an offer is made, it is always accompanied by one or more requests, whether implicit or explicit.

For example, the steak house's offer comes with requests to dress appropriately, leave your toddlers with a sitter, and pay the bill at the end of your meal. By contrast, the fast-food establishment's implied requests are to pay the bill *before* your meal and clear your own table when you're done eating.

In offering this book on the commercial market, my publisher and I have implied requests to purchase the book legally and not make unauthorized copies without our permission. In Table 23, there are some common examples you might encounter in your workplace.

Table 23 — An Offer a Day Keeps the Bosses at Bay

Offer	Request
We will complete the project in the next six months	If you provide us with milestone funding per the chart
We want you to speak at our next conference	Submit an abstract through our website
I can design a two-day workshop for your staff	But only if you pay me 50% in advance
We can increase your profit margins	You must provide us with your financial statements first
You can view our website for free	After you accept all our tracking cookies
We have an open house at our facility next week	You must register in advance
I have this great book about Telling it Like a TOPGUN	Purchase your own copy and please protect my copyright

Like the commutative property of addition, we can reverse the columns in Table 23 to produce the same effect in Table 24.

Table 24 — A Request a Day Keeps the Cobwebs Away

Request	Offer
Please continue funding our project	This will let us complete the project in 6 months
If you submit your abstract	We might offer you a speaking slot at our conference
If you pay me 50% in advance	I'll customize a two-day workshop for your staff
Show us your financial statements	So, we can find ways to increase your margins
By accepting these website tracking cookies	You'll have a better experience on our free website
Register in advance	To attend our open house next week
Purchase my book	And I'll teach you how to Tell It Like a TOPGUN

DROP THE MIC

Although I have saved this design section for last, it is hands down the most important step. Recall in Step 1 Purpose, you and your audience sacrificed your time, energy, and other opportunities to be at the appointed place and time of your presentation. In my view it is disrespectful to merely end with the obligatory "thank you." Rather, it is imperative that you review your purpose and make sure that the final slide in your deck ensures that your purpose is fulfilled.

The most powerful presenters consider every presentation as an opportunity for cooperation. Every speaker should share their gratitude with the audience. But instead of the common "thank you for listening," that you see in a typical Inform the Industry-type, one of my most often used signoffs is to say: "If you enjoyed this presentation, make sure to thank [so and so] for arranging for the two of us to be here together." This explicit request serves two purposes: it forces the listener to act instead of just walking away, and it elevates the identity of the person who coordinated the event.

At the end of a typical presentation, the speaker usually says something like: "Thank you and now I'll take your questions." This creates two problems. First is the expectation of applause after finishing the formal portion of the talk. If they clap wildly, you'll be in such a dopamine-infused state, you'll just want to walk off the stage then and there. If they don't clap at all, your mood might shift to anger. Neither mood serves you well as you begin the interactive phase. Better to be in a mood of wonder regarding what questions might arise.

Second, it's my experience that the first question after any talk is usually from a skeptic or "know it all" that wants to prove their own Dreyfus level of mastery in front of the crowd. You know the type. They first share a long monologue about their education and opinions before getting to their question, if at all. This shifts both the audience's mood from appreciation to "yeah, what about that?" and your mood towards defensiveness.

Third, and most important, is that questions rarely align with the presentation's purpose. Using the recency heuristic, you finished with a summary of your key points and then made your offer (or request). Audience questions will now override your priorities in the listener's limited short term memory stack.

The solution is to insert your "Any Questions?" slide about two or three slides before the end and preface it with the following script: "I still have my closing points to make but I'll pause here for any burning questions you may have."

No matter how off track the Q&A session gets, you retain the power to direct the listeners back to the center to achieve your purpose, not theirs. This also helps you to limit the Q&A to a reasonable time frame, again so as not to dilute the impact of your delivery.

By now you understand that your "drop the mic" moment should always be a request and/or an offer. In Table 25 are a few examples appropriate to the scenario you chose at the beginning of the design phase:

TABLE 25 — TACTICS FOR A STRONG FINISH

Scenario	Example Requests / Offers
Inform the Industry	Sign up for our newsletter, enroll in our program, connect with me on LinkedIn, follow me on … Here's my email, tell me what I got wrong. We're looking for partners to join this project, come see me during the break.
Pitch the Prospect	Can we set up a time next week to discuss this project in more detail? Can I book a time for you to visit our facility? Can I have my technical lead contact your PM to better understand your requirements?
Compel the Customer	When will you be able to sign the contract? Are you able to approve this project for the price indicated? Are there any concerns left that haven't been covered? We'd like to get started on Monday. Can you put me in front of the decision maker?
Persuade the PM	Accept and approve the status report. Approve the next phase of tasks and funding. Approve our request to make the recommended engineering changes. How can we make this project better? Now that we're complete, what comes next?

Let's see this in action in President Kennedy's Moon Speech. The purpose of his presentation, as with most political speeches, was to request support from his followers and perhaps even persuade some of his detractors. Throughout the talk he highlights all the offers and requests that come with landing on the moon (Part 3e):

- An offer to keep space from becoming a battlefield.
- Offer of new knowledge.
- Offer to grow the economy with new companies and jobs.

- Request to have the citizenry pay for the program*.
- Request for Rice University to continue to play a role.
- Of course, finishing it off with a request from his faith.

*Note: Towards the end of the speech, I love how the speech uses a highly common yet immensely effective sales technique called "*reduction to the trivial*" by equating the cost of the program to only 50 cents per week per person (~$5 today). Ethical manipulation? You decide.

As another example worth exploring, search for Steve Jobs' iPhone debut presentation from January 2007, not the short excerpts but the full 80-minute version. In my opinion, this is ***the*** most Tell It Like a TOPGUN talk I have ever seen. Of course, I'd encourage you to watch the entire talk and pick out the all the elements that you've learned from this book. But, for now, just fast forward to the final few minutes as he lays out the audience request to help him capture just 1% of the then 957 million-unit-per-year cell phone market by the end of 2008.

His call to action was obviously heard as the iPhone achieved almost 5% by the end of 2007![74] I wish all of us could have five times ROI from our presentations.

STORY TIME WITH GOLDY

For Dave's eulogy, my first thought was, other than emotional pleas to support the departed's loved ones or donate to a relevant charity, who the hell makes offers or requests at a funeral? How crass. This being no ordinary funeral, I thought it was vitally important to honor a conversation that Dave and I had during that once-in-a-lifetime evening I spent with him touring the launchpad two days before the launch.

At the same level as the shuttle's entrance hatch on launchpads, NASA had installed (and still has) an emergency egress system which allows the astronauts to get away from the shuttle as quickly as possible in the event of, say a fuel leak, or other threatening

74 https://www.statista.com/statistics/216459/global-market-share-of-apple-iphone/

situation.[75] Imagine a zip-line configuration that permits a fully dressed crewman to jump into a basket, slide a few thousand feet down to a protected bunker.

While Dave was explaining how the system worked and how he had to practice, he shared a far more prescient and intimate recognition of the true dangers he faced. Both of us were inculcated in the military aviation philosophy of investigating aircraft accidents from a safety first, retribution last objective. In a rather matter-of-fact tone, he said to me:

"Goldy. If anything were to happen to us, you know that I just want NASA to investigate it like we do mishap boards in the Navy. Do not try to fix blame on anyone. We all know how dangerous this is and we accept the consequences. Just fix the problem and get the program flying again."

Or words to that effect since, after all, it was 20 years ago as I'm writing this.

So that became the siren song of my speech.

I made one very explicit request to Administrator O'Keefe and Space Shuttle PM Ron Dittemore to, in accordance with Dave's wishes, investigate the cause, fix the problem, and get back into space (Part 3f, lines 115 – 117).

And, of course I made a more emotionally appealing request to the entire room. The implicit request throughout to remember Dave as a Renaissance Man and somebody whose gifts he gave to others could be a guide for our own gift giving.

75 See https://ntrs.nasa.gov/api/citations/20110012275/downloads/20110012275.pdf

MAKE AN OFFER CHECKLIST

While this is the shortest of the checklists, it is by far the most important.

MAKE AN OFFER (OR REQUEST)

1. Your purpose .... REVIEW AND ADJUST AS REQUIRED

During the design or rehearsal process of the presentation, the purpose originally intended from Step 1 may change. It is vital to review the purpose and opening slides and ensure the opening and closing thoughts are congruent.

2. Your offer/request .... CRAFT
3. Purpose and request / offer congruence .... CHECK

PART II

MISSION EXECUTION

STEP 7: PREP YOUR PLAN

By failing to prepare, you are preparing to fail.

~ Benjamin Franklin

We've now completed the mission planning phase of our presentation. Now it's time to prepare the room, audience, and yourself to Tell It Like a TOPGUN.

THE BATTLEFIELD

The goal of every presenter is to control, as much as possible, the distractions in the environment that will prevent your message from being heard. Contrary to popular media, our brains aren't capable of multitasking.[76] The listener's brain is easily distracted by sights, sounds, and smells. Recall from the *Us* versus *Them* discussion that the first thing the brain does with incoming stimuli is to check if it matches something it has encountered before. Your presentation is already something they've never seen or heard before. Therefore, it's important to mitigate all other incoming signals which will lead the brain to shift processing away from you and towards the distracting input.

For example, as I wrote the first draft of this section, the howling wind outside my office kept breaking my concentration while trying to place these perfect words on pixels. Funny how different I am now than my teen years when I couldn't stand to do homework unless I was listening to The Boss, The Who, or Yes.

Let's revisit our evolutionary biology and the five senses to help uncover the sources of distraction from the conference room to the lecture hall.

Because we're visual beings, what we are seeing is the likeliest source of distraction. One purpose of the rods in our eyes is to detect motion in our peripheral vision.

76 C. Rosen, "The myth of multitasking," *The New Atlantis,* 2008, 105-110.

You too have likely unconsciously shifted your gaze when spotting motion out the window of a conference room or when someone entered or left a lecture hall during the talk. Comedians revel in such opportunities to call attention to the distraction and shift their audience's (and perhaps their own) mood from disappointment to enjoyment.

Next up on our sensory hit parade is sound. In the wild, this too was part of our early warning network to focus our attention on threats that rustled leaves as they approached. From the lion's roar to the border collie's bark, we animals rely on our hearing as a survival tool. Again, you can reflect on your own experience with the annoying lawn mower outside, the squeaky a/c fan motor overhead, or the buzzing sound from the wall speakers.

Our sense of touch is yet another source of distraction. Perhaps not as quickly as vision or hearing, our bodies will react negatively over time to discomfort produced by our seats, room temperature, humidity, even our attire, such as when we're breaking in new shoes.

Our olfactory system is also in play. Territorial animals can immediately detect the odor of an interloper. Humans can be easily distracted by both positive and negative odors. The smell of fresh cookies in the back of the meeting room can elicit fond memories of cooking with grandma as a child. Somebody wearing strong cologne or perfume can trigger a happy recollection of a spouse or the disgust reaction of an ex-partner.

As for me, I enjoy a good cigar so, whenever I travel, I'm always on the lookout for the nearest cigar lounge. However, I never smoke with the clothes I intend to wear at my presentation, so as not to alienate non-smokers.

Lest you think I was going to leave out our sense of taste, fear not. But with a slight twist. In a rather disturbing finding from research conducted by Shai Danziger and colleagues at Ben Gurion University, they found that the outcome of parole hearings was influenced as much by the judges' eating habits as it was by legal argument.[77] Over the course of more than 1,000 hearings, the probability of a favorable ruling (from the prisoner's/parolee's perspective) steadily dropped from a high of ~65% to near zero towards the end of a session returning to that level immediately after a meal or snack break. While the jury is still out (pun intended) on the specific role

77 S. Danziger, J. Levav and L. Avnaim-Pesso. "Extraneous factors in judicial decisions" in *Proceedings of the National Academy of Sciences,* 108(17), 2011, 6889-6892.

of food versus cognitive overload as the culprit, there's no denying the role that fasting plays in becoming "hangry" (hunger + angry).

Table 26 below contains a non-exhaustive list of potential environmental distractions along with possible mitigation strategies.

Table 26 — Environmental Sources of Distraction

Distraction Sources	Mitigation TTPs
Location	Presenting at their location will make them feel more in control. At your facility might be intimidating – which can be good or bad depending on your desired outcome. **Inform the Industry:** Best done at home or neutral turf **Pitch the Prospect:** Their site **Compel the Customer:** Their site **Persuade the PM:** Your site
Layout	Whenever possible, arrange the room to minimize the listener's distraction and discomfort. For example, don't accept classroom style seating for a **Compel the Customer** situation. Ensure you'll be able to make eye contact with everyone at some point during the talk, which means walking around the room if necessary.
Seating	Avoid having seats near machinery (a/c units), doorways, behind posts. When in an intimate setting, try to sit side-by-side with the prime listener, or at a 90° angle to them. Avoid sitting opposite since it promotes an US vs. Them, adversarial relationship.
Lighting	Too bright or too dim can cause eye fatigue. If using a screen, avoid overhead lights that wash out the screen.
Cleanliness	Take ownership of the room's organization and state. Even if you must do it yourself, be sure the room looks as orderly and clean as possible.
Noise	Minimize all distracting noises, inside and outside. It's better to pause for a temporary interruption (siren, phone ringing) than to talk over it because your listener will be focused on the noise and not your signal.

Method	Don't immediately default to a digital presentation. Sometimes, no visual (think MLK's "I Have a Dream" or Kennedy's "Moon in this Decade" speeches). For more intimate settings (presenting to just a few individuals), using a handout makes them feel more in control as they can skip around as desired.
Handouts	Before: May reveal too much which produces boredom during the talk. During: Can be useful to delay the crowd while you're setting up. Can also be a distraction as listeners skip ahead. After: Helpful to leave a reminder of your talk to refer to. However, missed opportunity for listeners to make action-oriented notes on the slides (e.g., "This schedule seems too long, be sure to ask.")
Scheduling	Try to be the last or first presenter on the list. Last is most memorable (recency bias). First can set the bar (affinity bias). Middle is most forgettable. Present immediately after a meal or break to get the highest positive response (as one reporter summarized the Danziger report "Justice is served, even more so after lunch" yuk, yuk).

The key takeaway from this section: Be Goldilocks—not too cold, not too hot; not too loud, not too quiet; not too hard, not too soft; …

THE ONLINE BATTLEFIELD

Video teleconferencing has been around since the 1970s as a tool for large corporations, governments, and educational institutions, so there was plenty of evidence to develop industry TTPs for delivering an online speech by the time it became more mainstream in the 2010s. The global pandemic, however, produced a once in a generation (we hope no more frequently than that) opportunity for researchers and service providers to collect hundreds of millions of data points at every level of education and corporate interaction.

I try to keep up with the latest findings in adult learning theory and practice, yet I'm often confused by some of the conflicting conclusions. As a result, I reached out to Paul Zak and his team at Immersion Neuroscience for help.

He and his company have developed a software algorithm that leverages hidden signals in several cranial nerves to determine whether a participant is immersed, or not, by what they're viewing.[78] The magic of their product is that it works with more than a dozen commonly available heart rate monitors and smart watches.

So, while my participants' in-person delivery experience outperforms the online experience, the data I have been collecting from the immersion tool has reinforced much of what we in the public speaking industry had already concluded anecdotally. Here are few key highlights:

- Use two-way video as much as possible
  - Enhances trust building
  - Allows you to gauge captivation
- Good sound is more important than good video
  - We can tolerate or turn off fuzzy video
  - Poor sound can be fatiguing
- Look at your camera more than your monitor
  - Eye contact is even more important online
  - Don't use your monitor as a crutch for not knowing your material
  - Use a transparent camera mount (like Plexicam's) that puts your camera in the middle of your screen
- Less lecturing, more interaction
  - Allow interruptions during your talk, if possible
  - Leverage the use of "hand raise" tech or moderators
  - Periodically interrupt your own talking to ask a question of one or more audience members
- Virtual backgrounds are a mixed bag
  - Not using a virtual background is more authentic and trustworthy
  - Specific types of backgrounds are the most trustworthy[79]
    - Personal (books and plants) good

---

78 For more on the details of the technology, see https://www.getimmersion.com/

79 A. Cook, M. Thompson and P. Ross, "Virtual First Impressions: Zoom backgrounds affect judgments of trust and competence" in *PLoS ONE 18*(9), 2023, e0291444.

      - Outrageous backgrounds ... not so much
    - Fancy or overly stimulating images are distracting
    - Showing a pic that's not connected to your real life can be interpreted as disingenuous (untrustworthy)
    - Having a plain or consistent background no matter where you broadcast from can help eliminate distractions
- Assume some portion of your viewers are using small screens, and design your fonts, images, and slides accordingly

STORY TIME WITH GOLDY

Towards the end of my naval career, I was tasked with competing against my sister services to secure a $20M budget for a TTP development project at Fallon. In advance of the final selection board decision meeting, we had to individually present the details of our proposed idea to military and government civilian leaders.

I recall one of the leaders, an SES-3 (the civil service equivalent of a two-star admiral), had a strict protocol for all one-on-one briefings. We had to stand around a round "high-top" table (the kind you find in a bar), and brief to a paper copy of our slide deck. We were told that since most of us become fatigued after 15 to 20 minutes of standing, this was his purposeful strategy (as a Leader type on the LEFT scale) to ensure presenters were clear, concise, and quick.

THE LISTENER

Justice is what the judge ate for breakfast.

~ Judge Jerome Frank

Have you ever attended (or seen depicted in the movies) one of those motivational seminars selling investment strategies, entrepreneurship, or self-esteem? They invariably start every session with an absurdly upbeat rah-rah cheer with annoyingly loud, uplifting music in the background.

Why are those Pitch the Prospect-type presentations so successful at getting their audience to "just say yes" to purchasing their books, additional seminars, consulting services, or whatever? Because they're brilliant at orchestrating receptive moods.

As mentioned earlier, at the start of every presentation your listener is in one or more moods. For example, a Monday morning internal mood of "I can't listen to anything until I've had my morning coffee" is quite different from a pre-Happy Hour mood of "I wish this were over so I could head to the bar for some fruity Sex on the Beach" (a popular mixed drink, not anything else you might be thinking). Being mandated by your boss to read this book (quantity discounts available, just sayin') will likely put you in an entirely different mood than if a trusted colleague strongly recommended it. As your talk approaches the lunch hour, a "hangry" mood can set in.

With the emergence of portable cassette tape recorders (Gen Z readers, ask your grandparents to explain) in the late 1970s, the practice of playing high energy "fire-up" music at the start of and in between each lecture became the norm at TOPGUN. From Elward (2021, pg 189):

> [Dan] McCort said he used the 1968 classic "Fire" by Arthur Brown, which began with the distinctive line "I am the God of Hellfire!" for his 1v1 lecture, and the Beatles' "Back in the USSR" for his Alpha Strike lecture. "These were two of my favorites, given the nature of our business and the Cold War."

This was clearly an attempt to orchestrate a receptive mood, both for the instructor as well as the student.

As part of your preparation, you can review this list of restrictive moods in Table 27 to anticipate what might grip one or more listeners and then speculate on how you might be able to shift their mood to the relevant receptive counterpart.

Table 27 - Moods Я Us

Restrictive Moods	Receptive Moods
• Arrogance	• Respectful
• Boredom	• Curious
• Comfortable	• Perplexed
• Confusion	• Wonder / Inquiry
• Despair	• Enthusiastic
• Distrust / Skepticism	• Trust
• Fear / Anxiety	• Acceptance / Serenity
• Impatience	• Patience
• Overwhelm	• Ambitious
• Panic	• Confidence
• Resentment	• Responsible
• Resignation	• Resolution

In Table 28 are some examples for each of the four scenarios and a specific strategy I've successfully used in that situation:

Table 28 — Masterfully Managing Moods

Type	Possible Restrictive Moods	Strategies for Orchestrating Receptive Moods
Inform the Industry	Boredom	Start with an unexpected anecdote of a scary personal experience. [Transparency note: That's exactly what I did by talking about the eulogy at the very start of this book.]
Pitch the Prospect	Skepticism	Speak to an 'Us' connection up front. Include bona fides at the end.
Compel the Customer	Arrogance	Use a case study from a person or company they admire that found success with your product, service, or idea.
Persuade the PM	Impatience	Authentically accept blame for any delays. Acknowledge the facts that occurred and what you learned from the experience to prevent reoccurrence.

STORY TIME WITH GOLDY

For Doc's eulogy, I thought the mood would go well beyond the typical somber funeral.

He was the last of his crewmates to be memorialized so the mourning families and his NASA colleagues had already attended a string of such services. The venue was the chapel at Arlington National Cemetery with an honor guard and horse-drawn caisson stationed outside perched to march him to the burial plot. Furthermore, there was a national mood of "how could NASA have let yet another Shuttle crew die?" even before the full extent of its (mis)management had come to light.

However, in the weeks leading up to the speech, as I commiserated with others in Doc's sphere of influence, we all agreed that (a) he was not a mournful character and (b) he died living his dream of going to space. That naturally led me to open with humor—to let the assembled masses know right away that this was going to be a true celebration of our Renaissance Man and to join me in shifting their mood accordingly.

Besides mood, there are other physiological and psychological strategies for preparing an audience of any size. It's important to recognize that, without proper stimulation, most humans can't last more than twenty minutes, hence the reason TED Talks are limited to 18. In this modern, TikTok, YouTube, and Twitch-based world, some have even suggested a new norm of just twenty seconds (anecdotally, about how long my son pays attention to me before his eyes glaze over).

The TTPs and checklists I've already cited to Make it Personal, Make it Emotional, Make it Visual, and Make it Compelling, are all designed to lengthen the span. In Table 29 below, I've listed some additional considerations and their corresponding, attention-grabbing TTPs.

Table 29 — TTPs for Preparing Your Listener

Biology / Psychology	TTPs
Authority Gradient	People pay attention to authority figures. Counter-intuitively, an outsider (paid consultant) will wield more authority during their talk than an insider. As the presenter, like a TOPGUN instructor, you ARE the authority on your topic. The listener remains the authority on how best to employ your ideas in their specific situation.
First Impressions	Dress at or slightly above your listener's level. Too fancy and you'll be perceived as too far removed from their reality. Too casual and you'll lose their respect.
Hearing	Talking too softly will cause fatigue. Talking too loudly will be equally distracting. If using an interpreter (including sign language), talk more slowly than normal and insert sufficient pauses for the interpreter to keep pace.
Smell	Avoid using perfume/cologne. You may think you smell good, but you may remind a listener of a negative (or even a distractingly positive) experience. Never smoke or drink alcohol before presenting as the odor may turn listeners off.
Touch	ALWAYS produce a "hands-on" effect if you can do it safely. Listeners will feel a sense of "ownership" if they can have a kinesthetic connection. It increases memorability.
Bladder	At some point in a long presentation, listeners cannot concentrate on your content and, instead, start hoping for the next break—especially after morning coffee and afternoon lunch.

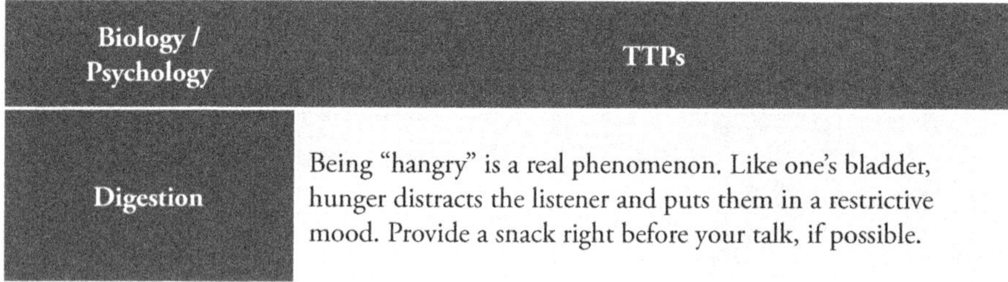

Biology / Psychology	TTPs
Digestion	Being "hangry" is a real phenomenon. Like one's bladder, hunger distracts the listener and puts them in a restrictive mood. Provide a snack right before your talk, if possible.

YOURSELF

> *Don't practice until you get it right. Practice until you can't get it wrong.*
>
> - Unknown

Sociologist, author, and public speaker Brené Brown wrote her first book in 2004. Her 2010 presentation titled The Power of Vulnerability is the fifth most viewed TED talk.[80] In her own words:

> People often ask me if I still get nervous when I speak in public. The answer is yes. I'm always nervous. Experience keeps me from being scared, but I'm still nervous. First, people are offering me their most precious gift—their time. Time is, hands down, our most coveted, most unrenewable resource. If being on the receiving end of one of life's most valuable gifts fails to leave you with a lump in your throat or butterflies in your stomach, then you're not paying attention.[81]

This is likely to sound counter to Dr. Brown's mantras for vulnerability and authenticity, but the truth is, when you're in front of the room, no matter the audience's size, you're an actor playing a role. Who you are in real life is not necessarily who you need to be when delivering your presentation. Watching her TED talk, you would never know how nervous she was.

---

80 https://www.ted.com/playlists/171/the_most_popular_ted_talks_of_all_time

81 Brene Brown, *Dare To Lead. Brave Work. Tough Conversations. Whole Hearts.* (Random House, 2018), xi.

As I keep reminding you throughout this book, your role is to ethically manipulate your listener for their own benefit. Even if you're the meekest of introverts at your desk, you must overcome your nature and "be a Vincent" (referring to the Cialdini excerpt on page 43-44).

I remember the first time I noticed this technique of fully transforming one's character. I was at mini boot camp (two weeks instead of eight) at the Great Lakes Naval Recruit Depot being yelled at by Gunnery Sergeant Poyner, a Marine's Marine, and a war-fighting veteran of the Vietnam Conflict (think R. Lee Ermey's outstanding portrayal of Gunny Hartman in *Full Metal Jacket*). Two weeks later, back at the ROTC unit on the college campus, Gunny was an entirely different man—relaxed, personable, approachable. The following year, there he was again, with that year's entrants—yelling, cursing, standoffish, intimidating. I had never seen such transformations. I concluded for myself that it had been an act of ethical manipulation designed to engender discipline, confidence, and teamwork in the most efficient and effective means. Brilliant.

I'm certainly not encouraging you to scream like a drill sergeant at your audience. Nor am I asking you to embrace the quintessentially boring persona of the economics professor in *Ferris Bueller's Day Off* (Ben Stein's "anyone, anyone"). But I am suggesting that you create your thoughtful persona regarding every aspect of your stage presence including your voice, hand and leg movement, facial expressions, and others, starting with Posture.

POSTURE

The second most viewed TED Talk is "Your Body Language May Shape Who You Are" by Amy Cuddy. A former assistant professor at both Northwestern's Kellogg School of Management (Go Cats!) and the Harvard Business School, she advocates the use of a "power pose"—raising your hands over your head in a v-for-victory shape, for a full two minutes, to make you feel more powerful prior to a meeting, interview, or talk. There's some controversy surrounding her findings, which she has acknowledged (see the notes on her talk.☺

https://www.ted.com/talks/amy_cuddy_your_body_language_may_shape_who_you_are).

For a less controversial set of recommendations on posture, read (or view) any body language book or online video of former Federal Bureau of Investigation (FBI) interrogator Joe Navarro, a recognized expert.[82] For an excellent overview of how to display confidence: https://youtu.be/VRJzvJ5XPQI

Stage Position: Whether in a room or on a stage, avoid being handcuffed to a podium. Standing behind such a monument reinforces Us versus Them and makes you seem less approachable. Obviously, also avoid standing directly in front of the screen. However, to emphasize a particular point, you can walk to the onscreen artifact and look at it, point to it, etc.

Voice: The best example of what not to do is the teacher in the previously mentioned Ferris Bueller's Day Off. A monotone style puts the listener's brain to sleep. Periodically change your pitch, volume, and rate to wake it up—especially when you want to highlight a particularly important point (like your Offer or Request).

Facial Expressions: As discussed earlier, we judge facial expressions in tens of milliseconds. As Todorov (2019) has proven, trustworthiness is one of the prime outcomes of these spot judgments, so learn how to promote a happy look.

> So if you want to be seen as happy—and hence, trustworthy—in your old age, smile more often now. As Parsons argued, the habits of the mind can find their way to the face, although it might take them considerable time to get there.[83]

Eye Contact: I am not a fan of the advice to "look above their heads." This is usually for those that are nervous to avoid feeling even more nervous when others are looking at you. I practice looking at a specific individual for no more than 4-5 seconds, then shifting my gaze to someone nearby. I try to make eye contact with as many people as possible in the room, but without rushing it. Here's a useful strategy that Dr. Brown uses:

> Even though it's just me onstage and possibly ten thousand people sitting in folding chairs in a convention center, I try to look into as many pairs of eyes as I can. … Even though it makes event production teams crazy, I always ask for the stage

82 L. Marusca, "What Every Body Is Saying. An Ex-Fbi Agent's Guide to Speed-Reading People" in *Journal of Media Research,* 7(3), 2014, 89.

83 Alexander Todorov, Face Value: *The Irresistible Influence of First Impressions* (Princeton University Press, 2017.

> lights to be at 50 percent. When they're at 100 percent, you can't see the audience at all, and I don't like talking into the void. I need to see enough faces to know if we're in sync. Are the words and images pulling us together or pushing us apart? Are they recognizing their experiences in my stories? People make very specific faces when they're hearing something that rings true for them. They nod and smile and sometimes cover their faces with their hands. When it's not landing, I get the side tilt. And less laughter.[84]

Movement: Pacing back and forth across a room or a stage is distracting. Movement should be purposeful. My strategy is to start on one side while looking at the eyes of those that are near me. Then, when the timing is right (after a few minutes) I'll deliberately walk across to the other side of the room (or stage) when what I'm saying is less important, but it allows me to see if heads are following me across the room—a sign of engagement.

Breath: Check out James Nestor's book or videos on how to improve your breathing techniques.[85] He has learned how specific sequences of deep or shallow breathing can promote more energetic versus more calming hormone production. If you're anxious and breathing too fast prior to your talk, you can use a calming technique. If you're hungover or exhausted, try one of the energetic exhalations.

Pace: One of the hardest things to master is your speaking speed. Too slow and the audience will lose interest. Too fast and they'll miss your message. You'll generally feel like your pace is glacial when, in reality, you're talking a mile-a-minute. Practice timing your talk.

Mood: Remember that moods are highly contagious. If you're not motivated by your own talk, don't expect your audience to be either. Pick one or more uplifting moods and try to stick with it (or them) throughout.

Emotion: Like actors, I encourage you to display various emotions throughout your talk. For one of the best examples of authentic emotionality (and mood setting), check out Steve Jobs' iPhone launch at MacWorld 2007 (more about this in Step 8).

---

84 Brown, *Dare To Lead,* xi.

85 J. Nestor, Breath: *The new science of a lost art* (Riverhead Books, 2020).

Hands: Use hand gestures to emphasize a learning point. Too many hand movements can be distracting. Avoid rubbing your hands together as if washing them, or crossing your arms, or putting each (or both) in your pocket. They're all signals of discomfort and lack of confidence. In my classroom work, this is where I ask the students to stand with their arms at their side, without fidgeting, while I drone on for a few minutes. In social settings, we're all so used to having a drink in one hand, crossing our arms, putting our hands in our pockets, etc., that having them just dangle at our side feels a bit uncomfortable at first. Try this for yourself the next time you're in a crowded social setting.

While we still have one more classroom module, you now have all the necessary TTPs to begin your rehearsal stages. Notice I said stages, plural. I didn't write this book for your run-of-the-mill talks at your monthly Rotary International meeting or for your sister's wedding toast. Tell It Like a TOPGUN should be used anytime you have a high consequence, "failure is not an option" type talk—where large sums of money are at stake or careers are made. Here are some commercial examples that would demand such dedicated peer review:

- New Product Launch (think Apple's unmatched presentations)
- Flight Readiness Review for a new aircraft or rocket
- Annual Report to Shareholders for a publicly traded company
- Courtroom opening and closing arguments
- Startup company's investor pitch (e.g., the Shark Tank)
- Nobel Prize acceptance speech
- TED Talk

For such occasions, I strongly encourage you to follow the process I am about to describe.

I SEE A MURDER BOARD IN YOU FUTURE

As I mentioned earlier, all the Navy weapons and tactics schools use a rigorous rehearsal mechanism before any instructor is permitted to teach in front of a class. Referred to as a "Murder Board", it is a multi-stage process of peer-reviewed rehearsals designed to fully prepare the instructor candidate for their first classroom experience.

This process has since been adopted well beyond the military, for example, by politicians preparing for debates.

Fast forward to my third and final tour as a weapons school instructor, the Naval Strike and Air Warfare Center (NSAWC) Instructor Manual (circa 1999) said:

> Though the name 'Murder Board' may sound intimidating, the purpose is not to 'blast' the instructor, but to critique and prepare him or her for that first class. Strict adherence to this process will ensure the best possible product for the instruction of the various NSAWC formal training programs.
>
> Murder Boards are designed to ensure that:
>
> Substantive content is as accurate and authoritative as possible.
>
> a. All NSAWC instructors are aware of what is being taught in all lectures.
>
> b. Duplication and redundancy is minimized.
>
> c. Instructor's techniques are as polished as possible.
>
> ...prior to the lecture being taught in a formal classroom situation."[86]

The murder board process occurred in three stages, each with an increasing level of formality and attendance as summarized in Table 30 below.

86 NSAWC, from 1999 – 2002 when I was there, was the parent organization to the three, then existing weapons schools—TOPGUN, Strike U., and CAEWWS.

Table 30 — Murder Board Stages

Stage	Description / Purpose / Outcome	Timing	Reviewers
Outline Murder Board	1st MB for a new lecture. Only the outline is reviewed to determine the instructor's accuracy and thoroughness of translating lesson requirements into lesson development direction.	Six Weeks Prior	Curriculum Review Board
Story Board Murder Board	2nd MB for a new lecture and 1st MB for a lecture when more than 1/3 of the content has changed. Review of the final ***draft*** of all slides and talking points. Like story boards in the film and TV industries, the slides don't have to be in their final "Gucci" form but mature enough to understand the graphic and textual components.	Four Weeks Prior	Curriculum Review Board
Content Murder Board	3rd MB for new content. 2nd for updated lecture, and the 1st MB for a new instructor taking over an existing lesson. Review of the final versions of all slides and talking points.	Two Weeks Prior	Entire Staff
Dress Rehearsal Murder Board	The final MB prior to being approved for presenting to a class of students.	One Week Prior	Entire Staff
Annual Review Murder Board	Review of lesson content checking for inconsistencies or duplications.	Anniversary of 1st Delivery	Instructor Staff

As mentioned in Elward (2021), we instructors under training (IUT) often conducted our own preboard practice sessions. Here are some additional NSAWC rehearsal TTPs that guided us:

- Practice six to ten times.
- Practice remembering ideas, not memorizing each word.
- It's okay to practice mentally, rather than aloud.

Side note: This is what high performing athletes regularly do. They visualize sinking the ninety-foot putt on the 18th hole, swishing a basket to make the game winning shot, landing a perfect dismount from the uneven bars in gymnastics.

- Rehearse from your note cards, not from a script.
- Practice only those gestures that reinforce a memorable item.
- Practice in front of a mirror.
- Practice the timing.
    - Practice pacing the delivery to land key points.
    - Not just to meet the time requirement
- Record and review your practice session

So, now you're in front of the room for your first murder board. What do you want the evaluators to evaluate? There are several templates for grading presentation rehearsals. A quick web search will uncover one of the more thorough templates by Toastmasters International.[87] For your historical entertainment, Figure 21 is the criteria that was used by NASA for the design review teams for what was to become the Space Shuttle.

87 At the time of this writing: https://toastmasterscdn.azureedge.net/medias/files/department-documents/education-documents/evaluation-resources/english/8053-generic-evaluation-resource.pdf

Murder Board: Project Team Recommendations
Evaluation Sheet

Use this sheet to guide your evaluation of the Project Teams's presentations. These scores will remind you how much each component persuaded you.

Shuttle	Not effective		Somewhat		Very effective
Thesis/argument	1	2	3	4	5
Evidence	1	2	3	4	5
Realistic/Doable	1	2	3	4	5
Politically Astute	1	2	3	4	5

Comments:

Satellites/Probes	Not effective		Somewhat		Very effective
Thesis/argument	1	2	3	4	5
Evidence	1	2	3	4	5
Realistic/Doable	1	2	3	4	5
Politically Astute	1	2	3	4	5

Comments:

Total Program	Not effective		Somewhat		Very effective
Thesis/argument	1	2	3	4	5
Evidence	1	2	3	4	5
Realistic/Doable	1	2	3	4	5
Politically Astute	1	2	3	4	5

Comments:

Privatization	Not effective		Somewhat		Very effective
Thesis/argument	1	2	3	4	5
Evidence	1	2	3	4	5
Realistic/Doable	1	2	3	4	5
Politically Astute	1	2	3	4	5

Comments:

FIGURE 21 - WHICH MB CAME FIRST: NASA'S CHICKEN OR TOPGUN'S EGG?

Did you notice the row for "politically astute" in each of the categories? Given the nation's waning interest in the Apollo program and Congress' desire to spend elsewhere, this was an entirely understandable criteria to be measured by in 1973. I find it fascinating to ponder if "politically astute" was, or should've been, a criteria used for the plethora of pandemic-related policy presentations.

For your purposes, Table 31 below is aligned with the TTPs I've introduced in this book.

Table 31 — Presentation Rehearsal Evaluation Tool

Component	Observations / Comments
Design Purposeful? Personal? Compelling emotional hook? Visual? Offer/Request?	
Delivery Prepared? Trustworthy (EARS)? Mood orchestrator?	
Style Verbal ticks ("um")? Body (language, movement, attire, etc.)? Voice (tone, rate, volume, infection)? Listener interaction (eye contact, able to handle questions)?	

One of the promises I made at the beginning of this book was to help you reduce your stage fright. I can tell you from my own personal experience and that of hundreds of my fellow Weapons School instructors, that coming out on the other side of the murder board process will absolutely produce the emotional fortitude you desire.

In the 2016 movie Sully, based on the true story of how US Airlines flight 1549 Captain Chelsey Sullenberger and First Officer Jeffrey Skiles piloted their dual-engine passenger jet to a safe landing in New York City's Hudson River, many remarked about the calmness of voice and demeanor from both crewmen.[88] Similarly emotionless remarks can be heard while listening to Apollo 11 Commander Neil Armstrong pilot his craft to a safe moon landing through multiple computer faults.[89] Or, in my opinion, the master of calm, United Airlines flight 232 Captain Al Haynes' communication with Air Traffic Controller Kevin Bachman as the crew fought their way down over the skies of Iowa in a crippled DC-10 that had lost all hydraulics.[90] We pilots are trained to be calm under stress by practicing dozens, perhaps hundreds of times in simulators with a "check pilot" evaluating us along the way.

General George Patton is famous for saying, "You fight like you train," which is why he trained his troops so hard. You want to reduce your stage fright? Rehearse, rehearse, rehearse.

With one caveat. Retired TOPGUN Instructor Vincent "Jello" Aiello had an interesting reaction to a Marine Topgun instructor's presentation when he first went through the syllabus as a student.

> The instructor was so polished, his lecture so flawless, that it actually had the opposite effect on me: I sat mesmerized, waiting for him to make even the slightest mistake or slip. Nothing. He was a machine.[91]

Perfection became a distraction for Jello, made the presenter seem like a "machine." This is something to avoid at all costs because it will definitely put you in the **Them** group. Be your authentic self, even if it means slipping up from time to time.

---

88 America West Airlines flight 1549 (note America West callsign is "Cactus 1549": https://youtu.be/yVCeQ89BB_o

89 Apollo 11 https://www.youtube.com/watch?v=RONIax0_1ec

90 United Airlines Flight 232 ATC Recording https://www.youtube.com/watch?v=-3YkiMDS5y8

91 https://www.fighterpilotpodcast.com/musing/how-to-present-like-a-Topgun-instructor/

PREPARATION CHECKLISTS

PREPARE THE ENVIRONMENT

1. Determine optimum location .... SELECT

NOTE

When you have the choice of where to deliver the talk, know that specific locations send subtle psychological signals. Your site means more power for you and less for your customer. Vice versa if at their site. Refer to Step 7 for more information.

2. Seating layout for maximum interaction .... SET
3. Appropriate lighting .... SET

Ensure the lighting is bright enough for the audience to take written notes if appropriate, but not so bright that it washes out the screen or prevents you from seeing their faces. If able, turn down or out lights in the front of the room while keeping the back of the room well lit.

4. Clean and organized .... CHECK
5. Distracting ambient noise .... MITIGATED
6. Handouts .... CHECK

NOTE

Carefully consider your strategy for handouts. Beforehand and they might become a distraction as some listeners will want to thumb ahead. Waiting until the end may impact relevant notetaking ability.

7. Timing/scheduling .... FIRST or LAST

WARNING

For talks given as part of a sequence of many, choosing to be first is optimum since it will (a) catch the audience at their freshest state and (b) set the bar high for others. Going last is most memorable because of the recency bias.

PREPARE YOUR AUDIENCE

1. Mood .... ANTICIPATE
2. Authority gradient .... HIGHER
3. Attire .... DETERMINE NORM
4. Somatosensory engagement .... DEMO GEAR
5. Bio breaks .... SCHEDULED
6. Food / snack breaks .... SCHEDULED

PREPARE YOURSELF

1. Attire .... SLIGHTLY ABOVE NORM
2. Odors .... AVOID MALODOROUS

Avoid smoking, drinking, and foods that can cause foul odors.

3. Voice .... EXPRESSIVE
4. Facial expression .... TRUSTWORTHY
5. Posture .... CONFIDENT
6. Eye contact .... CONSTANT SCAN
7. Stage position .... SET
8. Pockets .... EMPTY
9. Pointer .... STOWED UNTIL REQUIRED

STEP 8 — EXECUTE & DEBRIEF

I have it all together, I just forgot where I put it.

~ Unknown

Performing is very much like cooking: putting it all together, raising the temperature.

~ Pianist David Tudor

THE D-DAY AFTER TOMORROW

I can't help myself. The night before a class or a consequential presentation, I can rarely sleep. I am so strung out on dopamine, in anticipation of the sheer enjoyment I derive from delivering my best content, that getting as much as three hours of sleep is considered victory. That is not a recommended TTP. Both your family doctor and I recommend your daily dose of 7-8 hours rest.

There's near unanimity against operating motor vehicles and heavy equipment under the influence of alcohol. Worldwide, pilots are similarly restricted from imbibing within so many hours of piloting an aircraft.

A large body of corroborated research has concluded that sleep deprivation is the cognitive equivalent of being drunk. Hence the recommendation that to truly Tell It Like a TOPGUN requires a certain amount of preparatory discipline above that which you or your employer would normally expect. You should make it a standard practice to fence off at least twelve hours prior to your delivery to eat and sleep well, unmedicated.

STORY TIME WITH GOLDY

(Rated M for Mature Audiences Only)

In aviation (both military and civilian), there's a prohibition of consuming alcohol within 8 hours of a flight (the exact timing varies by regulatory authority). As an admonishment memory tool, all flight crew are taught the catchy saying: "8 hours from bottle to throttle."

In the late 90s, I was instructing at the Navy's School of Aviation Safety in Monterey, California (since moved to NAS Pensacola), teaching squadron safety officers and senior leaders the fundamentals of how to investigate and prevent aircraft accidents. This was also around when the US Federal Aviation Administration (FAA) started mandating that commercial operators develop their own Safety Management Systems (SMS). In the spirit of public-private partnerships, we made one seat per class available to the major airlines (Delta, United, American, etc.).

At about this same time, March 27, 1998, to be exact, the first erectile dysfunction (ED) medicine hit the market. Within a few months, anecdotal evidence emerged that a side effect of the redirected blood flow led to a reduction in the ability to discern the colors blue and green, especially at night. With glass cockpit technology and the display screens relying on the use of blue and green fonts, one of our commercial airline pilots (I believe from United) told us the FAA had published an Advisory Circular that cautioned pilots not to take ED meds within 6 hours of a night flight.

Well...

... like any halfway decent evening talk show host worth their salt...

... one of us just couldn't let the opportunity to coin yet another catchy, slightly more colorfully suggestive admonition.

Thus, was birthed, "Six hours from cumin' to goin'."

H-HOUR IS HERE

Regarding your attire, this was something I noted incorrectly depicted in both Top Gun movies. So as not to create too wide an authority gradient between instructor and student, we never wore "ribbons" (the colorful fabric showing off our "been there, done that"-ness) above our left breast pocket when instructing. Rather, we either wore our khaki uniforms with just our rank and nametag or we wore flight suits, producing a certain egalitarian atmosphere.

I remember the cautionary note I was given the day before my first acrobatics mission in flight school: "Don't eat anything you don't want to see coming back up in the middle of a barrel roll." Best advice I ever got.

The same warning applies here. Eat just enough to avoid becoming "hangry," but not to excess, and stay away from exotic or gas-producing foods. Certain foods are so spicy that your pores will literally exude sulfur-containing gases—I'm talking to you curry and Korean.

If you have time, take one last pass through your notes and slide deck. Again, it's not about memorizing words but rather your ideas. It can also be useful to note something relevant from a recent news report that can be woven into your narrative to further drive home a particular idea.

This may sound obvious, but plan to arrive well before the appointed hour to give yourself a travel buffer as well as an opportunity to make sure all the audio-visual equipment and any props are working properly.

Lastly, ***bring a colleague*** to take notes as depicted in Figure 22. If in a large hall, have them sit on one side or the other, near the wall about halfway back so they have a good view of the entire room. If presenting in a small conference room, have them sit against the wall so they have good visibility across the entire room.

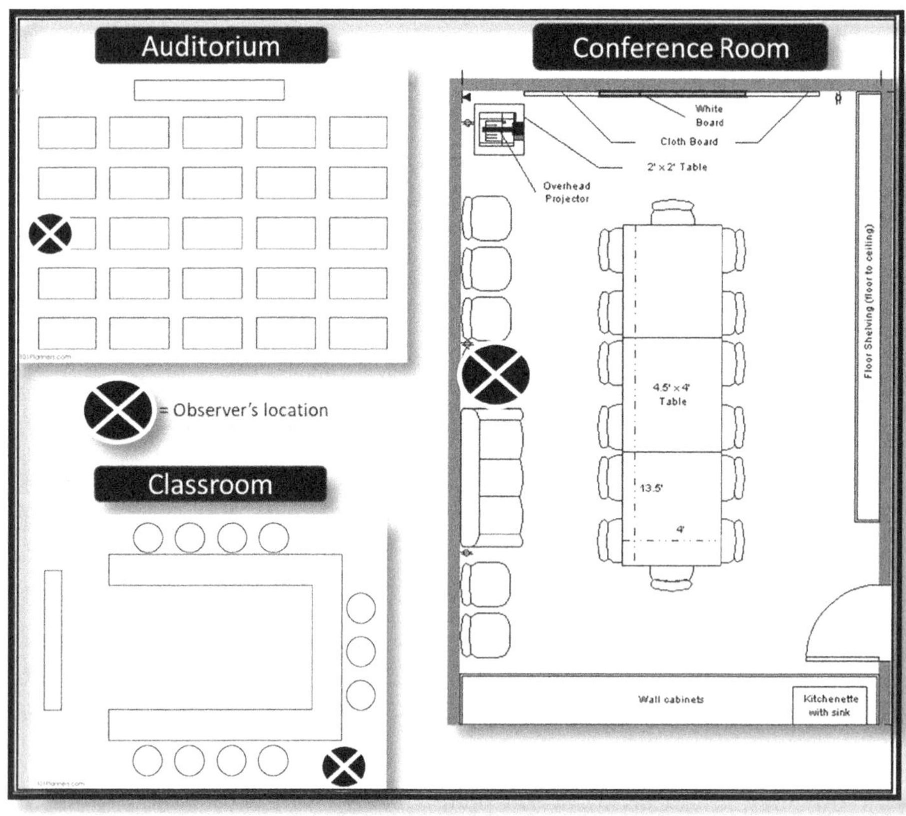

FIGURE 22- WHERE'S WALDO ... THE OBSERVER

FIRST ONE TO THE CHALKBOARD WINS THE DEBRIEF

When debriefing after things go wrong, ensure you have a developmental intent. Focus on learning and improvement,

NOT blame,

NOT judgment,

and certainly NOT punishment.

~ Psychologist Rob Yeung

By now, you probably know (or have surmised) that every military mission, no matter the nation or the service has an identical set of steps of execution:

1. Mission Planning
2. Mission Briefing
3. Mission Execution
4. After Action Review (a.k.a. Debriefing)

Steps 2 and 4 are so crucial to the development of a TOPGUN graduate that there's an entire classroom module titled … you guessed it … Briefing and Debriefing. As the Yeung quote suggests, the goal of the debrief is to eliminate emotion and ego in an incessant drive towards improvement. Back in the day before instrumented ranges and gee whiz replay systems: Students were instructed to draw their diagrams on the blackboard using colored chalk on the basis of the diagrams drawn on their kneeboards.[92]

The old joke, reflecting the highly competitive nature of flying fighter jets, then became: "First one to the chalkboard wins the debrief."

Side note: a kneeboard is a rigid platform strapped to an aircrew's thigh with sheets of paper on it for taking notes, so technically it should be called a thighboard, but I digress.

Today, the training ranges are all instrumented, and aircraft are equipped with recording equipment, so it's much harder to cheat … I mean

---

92 Elward, *TOPGUN,* 190.

… slant the debrief in the favor of the first arriving on the scene. Aircrew now debrief in large auditoriums with sophisticated displays and consoles.

THE DEBRIEF

Whether your mission is actual combat or peacetime training, debriefing is a vital component. Once again, "we fight like we train" to improve future performance.

Now that you've completed your mission execution—delivered your presentation—it's time to conduct your Debrief. The weapons schools use the mnemonic FATT to distinguish the elements of a proper debrief:

- Facts: What, where, and when did something happen.
- Analysis: Was your action a good or other-than-good* thing to have done?
- Tapes: Show the replay from multiple perspectives.
- Teaching: What are the lessons learned for future missions?

*The analysis is always summarized by having two columns up on the whiteboard labeled "Goods" and "Others." Why not Goods and Bads, you ask? That was a specific strategy by early TOPGUN Instructor Willie Driscoll who felt that saying the word bad to highly competitive fighter pilots would trigger a restrictive learning mood (Elward, p. 191). By the early 70s, the phrase stuck and, in typical fashion, the list of Goods is usually much smaller than the Others. That's to be expected since the goal is to focus on improvement not status quo.

In the first movie, TOPGUN instructors were depicted as flying against the students. That's only half the truth. While weapons school instructors fly in an "adversary" role on training flights, the primary instructor remains on the ground in the training range's "command center" where they can observe all the aircraft from an overhead, a.k.a. "God's Eye" view.

My point is that to truly debrief your presentation, it's best to let somebody else, somebody who had the God's Eye view, lead the debrief. This is why I recommended earlier in this Step bringing an observer along with you to every high consequence presentation. They're there to take the same notes as if it were a murder board, with the added responsibility of observing the audience. Below is a list of just some of the observations to be made:

- Who was engaged, leaning forward in their chair?
- Who was bored, disinterested, fiddling with their phones?
- Who sat where?
- What does that say about their status?
- Was a decision maker present?
- Did they indicate who they rely on most from their entourage?
- Which slides produced the most favorable audience reaction? Least?
- Who was taking vociferous notes?
- Who had questions? What were the questions?

This list is not all-inclusive. Over time, you and your colleague will learn what's most important for your future success.

It is also the case that many Inform the Industry type presentations, live and online, are recorded and posted to the host's website. This provides a valuable addition to the debrief as both you and your observer can stop the recording and analyze the details.

THE SIN OF A DECLINE

So, what happens if at the end of your talk, you don't achieve your outcome (e.g., your offer or request is declined)?

We've arrived at ***my #2 most important takeaway from this entire book*** (the first being the use of Freytag's Pyramid and learning how to be a great storyteller).

You have two options at this point: (a) "Oh well" and move on … or … (b) perform a diagnostic.

I call the diagnostic The SIN of a Decline because it forces you to examine the source of the decline:

- **S** for Situation:
  - Is the listener's current situation and mood conducive to accepting your offer / request?
  - Obviously, during COVID lockdown, nearly all my clients declined my offers for onsite training.

- **I** for Individual:
    - Was the individual gripped by a restrictive mood? Are they generally open to offers / requests?
    - There are many "Lone Ranger" types who think they never need anyone else's help. Avoid making offers / requests to these individuals.
    - Also avoid permanent skeptics and risk avoiders who never want to get involved with anything new.

- **N** for Narrative:
    - If the answer to the first two are fine, then likely your narrative was off. It didn't truly address your listener's concerns.

The point of this diagnostic is to recognize that just because the listener declined your request in this moment, it may be possible to re-engage in the future when the situation changes, the individual's mood has shifted, and/or the narrative has been crafted to be more compelling. In any case, properly diagnosing the SIN will help you learn valuable lessons in preparation for your next presentation.

DEBRIEF CHECKLIST

DEBRIEF

1. Presenter's notes .... GATHERED
2. Observer's notes .... GATHERED
3. Audience surveys, if possible .... GATHERED
4. Any recordings, ... GATHERED
5. Goods .... LIST
6. Others .... LIST
7. If Declined, perform diagnostic .... SIN
    a. Situation
    b. Individual
    c. Narrative

PART III

MISSION ADMIN

THE WEAPONS SCHOOL WAY

The challenge of education is not to prepare for success, but to prepare him for failure.

~ Vice Admiral James Stockdale, Congressional Medal of Honor awardee

Although the material in this appendix is not taught in my workshop, many of my civilian friends who reviewed early drafts encouraged me to include it.

Understanding TOPGUN requires an understanding of naval aviation. The United States Navy has the most sophisticated portfolio of aircraft and aircrews in the world. Operating day and night, in all weather, from every international body of water, flight crews are launched into the air by catapults that accelerate their planes from 0 to 140 knots (~160 mph or 260 kph) in a mere two and a half seconds. A few hours later, they're "trapped" aboard the carrier by the thinnest of margins (mere feet, actually), using a tailhook to catch a wire that slows the plane from landing speed to standstill in less than 700 feet (213 meters) of runway that's continuously moving away from you and heaving up, down, and sideways with the waves.

There are four categories of aircraft on a Navy carrier:

- Strike Fighter: FA-18E/F Hornets and F-35 Lightning IIs
- Electronic Warfare (EW): EA-18G Growlers
- Early Warning, Command and Control: E-2D Hawkeyes
- Sea Combat and Airlift: MH-60 Seahawk helicopters

I was not a pilot, rather I was a Naval Flight Officer (NFO), the guy that sits in the backseat, operates the weapons systems, and says stuff to the pilot like "Now make the houses bigger on the left and smaller on the right" and "That's a good boy, you did it."

I primarily flew in E-2 Hawkeyes managing the radar, voice and data communications, and other electronic equipment—"The rest is classified, so if I tell you, I'll have to kill you." As the electronic eyes of the battle group, we always launched first and landed last. In between, we used our surveillance equipment to not only monitor millions of cubic miles of airspace but also the land and sea surface in a constant effort to distinguish among friend, foe, and neutral.

It's important to understand that Top Gun is not just a Hollywood dramatization of a real United States military organization that helped flip the outcome of air-to-air combat more than fifty years ago over the skies of Vietnam. While historians can decide the laudability of that conflict, the many lessons of professionalism, devotion to teamwork, and skill craft that TOPGUN instructors and students exuded have since been applied to many high-consequence occupations such as hospital operating rooms, oil and gas drilling platforms, construction, and even finance.

A BRIEF HISTORY OF **TOPGUN** TIME

From 1959 to 1973, the US involvement in the Vietnam conflict had all the markings of modern-day nation-state warfare but was technically an undeclared "police action" (even though no police were involved). In 1964, the US Congress avoided a formal war declaration for political reasons, instead giving then President Lyndon Johnson authority to greatly expand US military presence there. Midway through the conflict, both the Navy and Air Force were suffering unexpected and unsustainable loss rates from air-to-air engagements with the enemy. While both services studied the problem, they came to somewhat different conclusions.

The Navy's response was to establish the Naval Fighter Weapons School (a.k.a. TOPGUN) in 1969 as a graduate school equivalent for specially-selected fighter aircrewmen. Only men at the time, as women were legally restricted from serving in combat aviation units until Congress changed the rules in the mid-90s. Hence the lack of female aircrew in the first Top Gun movie in marked contrast to the sequel.

The "gun" part of the nickname comes from the historical reference to combat aircraft having machine guns to shoot down enemy airplanes. Just like practicing at a shooting range, both Navy and Air Force fighter pilots practice shooting at a target that's being towed by another aircraft (I wouldn't want to be in that airplane, would you?). The pilot with the best score on the airborne target was hailed as the top gunfighter.

Beginning from rather austere circumstances in a stolen trailer (true story) at Naval Air Station Miramar in San Diego, California, a small group of hand-picked crewmen and an intelligence officer crafted a syllabus and commenced training other crews. It was recognized early on that only highly-qualified instructors would command the attention of top-tier students. Instructor selectivity bred prestige which further promoted selectivity, which enhanced prestige … in a virtuous cycle of constant improvement such that today, those who are privileged to wear the TOPGUN Instructor patch on their flight suits are revered not just by fellow naval aviators but are somewhat on par with the esteem earned by SEALS and Green Berets.

Some of the prevailing characteristics of a TOPGUN instructor's presentations are:

- Unquestioned, specialized expertise in their assigned topic
- Trained in instructional systems design and adult learning methods
- Presentations from memory without the use of notes
- Certifying each instructor through a series of Murder Boards[93] to fellow instructors
- Constant improvement because of changing tactics, technology, and student feedback

The results for the Navy were both immediate and stunningly positive. After a two-year hiatus to support peace talks, when air combat resumed in 1970, the Navy measured a near 600% improvement in "kill ratio" (a metric that compares the number of enemy aircraft shot down to each Navy aircraft lost). This was directly attributed to the efforts of the TOPGUN staff to propagate their teachings throughout the fleet via the graduates.

As mentioned earlier, the Air Force had diagnosed and addressed the kill ratio issue differently and thus saw a slight worsening post 1970. That's why they don't deserve to have a movie. Just sayin'.

Fast forward to 1983 when the Navy conducted an ill-fated airstrike into Lebanon in retaliation for a terrorist strike on a US Marine barracks.

93 "Murder boards" were supposedly invented by NASA and adopted / adapted by TOPGUN as a rigorous process to ensure every instructor meets the same quality standard. Details of how to use this process to rehearse your presentation are explained in Step 7.

One A-6 Intruder was shot down, leading to the pilot's death and the NFO's capture by Syrian forces, as well as the loss of an A-7 Corsair. The pilot was successfully recovered. Recognizing the historical parallel to TOPGUN's legacy from Vietnam, in 1984 the Navy created a second aviation weapons school called the Naval Strike Warfare Center, nicknamed "Strike U."

While they also got a patch, unfortunately for those of us privileged to wear it, it failed to garner the same level of interest from single women at the Officer's Club. (Don't ask me how I know this to be true). The good news is that at least their staff didn't have to learn how to sing "You've Lost That Lovin' Feeling."

Just four years later in 1988, recognizing the critical role that the E-2 Hawkeye aircraft plays for carrier aviation, the Navy created its third aviation weapons school, complete with its patch (I recommend averting your eyes), the Carrier Airborne Early Warning Weapons School, nicknamed "TOP DOME" after the circular radar dome that sits on top of the Hawkeye.

BETTER THAN A BRO

Although I never served on the TOPGUN staff, I did one tour at TOP DOME (1988 – 1990) and two tours at Strike U (1992 – 1995 and 1999 – 2002). At TOP DOME, I was what the Navy calls a "plank owner" because I helped establish the organization (think of laying the planks on a wooden ship). To help design TOP DOME into the image of its siblings, I had to intensely study and be trained in the same instructional methods.

In the early days, these three organizations were separate entities on two bases—TOPGUN and TOP DOME at Miramar and Strike U. at Fallon Naval Air Station in northern Nevada, ninety minutes east of Lake Tahoe (alternatively, arrive at Las Vegas, turn north and drive seven hours without seeing barely another human). In 1996, the three became one, co-locating in Fallon. Some number of years after I retired, two more weapons schools were added—SEAWOLF for the H-60 Seahawk community, and HAVOC for the EA-18G Growlers.

That's a ton of word salad I just fed you. To help see how the individual pieces fit together, the Figure 23 below summarizes the structure of Naval Air Warfare Development Command (NAWDC) as it exists today. A two-star admiral is the CEO equivalent of the organization. On the left are the staff functions that support the command's mission. The two primary instructional components I've been telling you about are the four aircraft type-specific weapons schools (middle) and the airwing integrated training department (right).

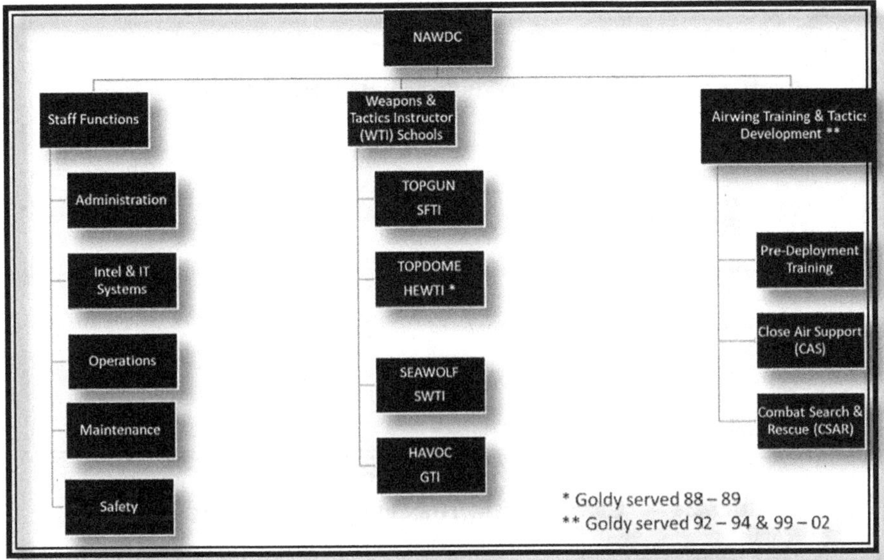

FIGURE 23 — THE WEAPONS SCHOOL FAMILY TREE

The Navy, like all the Services, has a pre-deployment training cycle that prepares the men, the women, and their equipment for operational deployments anywhere in the world. Since armed conflict can occur with little advanced warning, it is important that all forward deployed soldiers, sailors, airmen, and Marines always have the highest state of readiness. While the effectiveness of the US military is often attributed to the technological superiority of our gear, the truth is that our success is more a result of our realistic training.

Both Top Gun movies glossed over the full composition of a US Navy Carrier Strike Group (CSG) which includes more than just an aircraft carrier and its embarked airwing. A CSG also includes one or two cruisers, a few destroyers, supply ships, and an attack submarine or two. All told, about 7,500 personnel. To prepare the CSG for combat readiness, a complex series of evolutions occurs over the course of approximately twelve months, depending on world affairs and domestic politics. As Figure 24 shows, a CSG returns from a typical six-month deployment and, for the first month or so, enters a stand-down phase where sailors take some time off to spend with their families while equipment is fully inspected to determine what parts need to be ordered or upgraded.

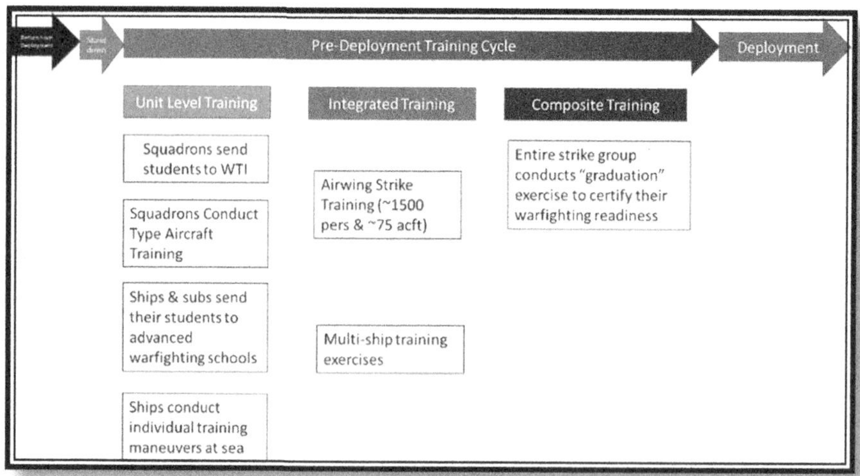

Figure 24 — Crawl, walk, then run toward deployment

Once the baby-making and hangovers have subsided, the pre-deployment training cycle begins with unit level training. As the diagram depicts, this is when squadrons identify their "best of the best" and send them off to the various weapons schools for their graduate school training. Meanwhile, the rest of the squadron is getting back to basics and training up any FNGs (that's military lingo for fucking new guy). At the same time as the flyboys and girls (a.k.a. "brown shoes"[94]) are doing their unit training, the crews on the ships and subs (a.k.a. "black shoes") are doing their own unit level training.

Many months later, the entire airwing is ready to come together and re-learn how to fly and fight as an integrated team. That's when they all arrive at Fallon for their mandatory airwing training lasting several weeks. The Fallon training is further divided into three phases—Mission-level, Integrated, and Advanced. The Airwing Training Instructors are, therefore, also somewhat integrated in that each of them has particular expertise from their specific aircraft type. But unlike the individual weapons school

94 For more on the history of why aviators are called Brown Shoes, see https://thebrownshoes.org/whence-term-brown-shoes

instructors, Airwing Training Instructors are groomed to understand the entire complexity of what the Navy calls an "Alpha Strike"—a large package of aircraft designed to strike multiple targets in enemy territory. The composition of an Alpha Strike from a single carrier can include two or three dozen aircraft, sometimes the entire complement of topside aircraft. During Operation Desert Storm, on the first night of combat operations in the Red Sea, we launched an Alpha Strike that consisted of planes from three carriers!

As an Airwing Training Instructor, referred to as "Overalls" for our overall awareness of the bigger picture (yeah, not very imaginative, I know), I take pride in having qualified to stand up in front of an entire room full of aircrew and intelligence officers from every type of aircraft, along with their commander, and deliver a concise summary of their "goods" and "others" (avoiding the use of the word "bad" for psychological reasons), with the list of others being often much longer than the goods. So yeah, TOPGUN instructors have their movies, but we Overalls have bigger…uh…evaluation forms.

To be fully transparent, having multiple instructor tours is not career enhancing. From Elward,[95]

> … the wisdom and experience of O-4s is needed and should be encouraged, rather than frowned upon by the Navy. For years, those who returned to TOPGUN for a second tour were often rolling the dice with their careers and gambling that serving two tours in the same place would not be a check mark against them as they aspired for command.

In the words of that great stooge and sage Curly Howard: "I resemble that remark."

Towards the end of my first Strike U. tour and second weapons school tour (by including my earlier TOP DOME tour), I had a heart-to-heart with my commanding officer where we concluded my odds of promotion past the rank of O-4 (lieutenant commander) were essentially nil. That was an emotionally freeing moment because it helped me shift my thinking from educator as avocation to vocation. Fortunately, the Navy (mostly) supported my newfound strategy allowing me to serve twice more in

---

95 Elward, *TOPGUN,* 510.

instructor roles—once at the Naval Postgraduate School and a final tour back in Fallon at the "new and improved" Strike U. I have no regrets over my career choices and can now proudly claim that I am probably the only military officer of any service to have served a total of five instructor tours.

A DAY IN THE LIFE

While the syllabus for each weapons school is obviously tailored to the specific characteristics of their platform and its mission, the general structure is roughly the same. There is a daily rhythm that includes one or more classroom lectures followed by either a simulator or live flight to practice what was just learned. For every flight, there's also the pre-mission planning time plus the post-mission debrief. All-in-all, for every one hour that Maverick spent in the air fulfilling his "need for speed," he spent four–six hours in ground school.

During the first few training missions, the instructors often lead to set the proper example for the students. Shortly thereafter, the students are responsible for all planning, executing, and debriefing of the mission.

You will find this akin to many science and engineering courses you may have taken in high school or college where each week contained both lectures and lab work. As you advanced in your coursework, you became more independent in the lab. As I mentioned in the Introduction, I am taking a similar approach in this book. I'll start each new section with fundamental academics needed to complete your lab work (e.g., designing your presentation). As both an engineer and a weapons school instructor, I stick to a scientifically rigorous approach to academics, hence the role of my neuroeconomics framework as the foundation for our work together.

HERE A CHECK, THERE A CHECK, EVERYWHERE A CHECK-CHECK

Aircrew, military and civil, live and die by checklists. As the name implies, a checklist is about complying with "a list of things to be checked or done." (Thanks for that incredibly helpful definition, Merriam-Webster).

Historians cite the crash of Boeing's B-17 prototype, the Model 299, on October 30,1935, as the impetus for checklists. During a demonstration test flight for the US Army Air Corps, a mechanically sound aircraft rolled down the runway at Wright Field in Dayton, Ohio, briefly climbing before crashing, killing two with three survivors. The accident investigation revealed that the flight crew merely forgot to release the gust locks (devices to keep the flight controls from being moved by wind gusts while parked and not operating). Boeing correctly surmised that overcrowded cockpits full of controls, dials, push buttons, circuit breakers, and instruments had become too complex to rely on fallible human memory to properly configure the aircraft from engine start to "don't you dare get out of your seat while we taxi to the gate."

Checklists have since found their way from military and commercial cockpits to maintenance procedures (e.g., engine inspections, tire rotations), passenger cabin crew stations (e.g., ovens, entertainment systems, coffee makers), and to other industries from manufacturing to medical. An oft-cited phrase in naval aviation is "checklists are written in blood" because modifications to checklists are made following recommendations from accident investigation boards, particularly when injuries or deaths had occurred. A typical flight checklist has a section devoted to each phase of flight and contains perhaps a dozen or more steps in each section. A table of contents might look something like this:

1. Walkaround Inspection
2. Pre-Start
3. Post-Start / Taxi
4. Takeoff
5. Climb
6. Cruise
7. Descent
8. Landing
9. Shutdown

Here's a real-life example checklist from the now decommissioned fleet of A-6E Intruders I used to fly at Strike U (for reference, see 1991's far less popular movie *Flight of the Intruder* no fault of Danny Glover or Willem Dafoe).

****

POST-START

1. BOOST PUMP TEST button .... DEPRESS
2. Anti-g valve .... PRESS TO TEST
3. VENT SUIT AND CUSHION AIRFLOW .... ADJUST
4. OXYGEN switch .... ON
5. Oxygen mask .... ATTACHED
6. Contact analog switch (KA-6D) .... ON
7. Rain Removal .... CHECK

The rain-removal system shall be checked by actuating the windshield switch to the AIR position and by holding your hand over the top of the windscreen to feel the hot air. Turn the windshield air off as soon as possible to prevent cracking the windshield. If unable to turn off the hot air, secure the engines as soon as possible.

8. NWW BLEED-AIR isolation valve switch .... CHECK
9. RADAR ALTIMETER .... ON AND SET
10. LOX/FUEL/OIL .... TEST
11. Canopy .... CLOSED
12. ADI .... ON AND ADJUST
13. MAN/RAM air switch .... HOLD
14. AIR CONDITIONING COCKPIT switch .... OFF
15. AIR CONDITIONING COCKPIT switch .... ON
16. MAN/RAM AIR switch .... COLD/HOLD

NOTE:

Placing the MAN/RAM AIR switch to COLD, then HOLD should prevent 700°F bleed air from being introduced into the cockpit if the dual temperature control valve fails during run up for takeoff.

17. ECM .... OFF UNTIL AIRBORNE

****

Notice the "**CAUTION**" box after step 7 and "Note" after step 16. Throughout most every aircraft's operating manual, there are three types of supplemental headers:

- **WARNING:** An operating procedure, practice, or condition, that may result in injury or death if not carefully observed or followed.
- **CAUTION:** An operating procedure, practice, or condition, that may result in damage to equipment if not carefully observed or followed.
- **Note:** An operating procedure, practice, or condition, essential to emphasize.

[Sheesh, A-6 checklist, thanks for telling me about that 700°F bleed air. Reminds me of summers in Phoenix.]

This is why I have placed a checklist at the end of every Step in my process as a memory jogger to help you apply the TTPs I had just covered. Section 3G, later in this part, is a collection of all the checklists which I have also made available on the book's website (www.tellitlikeatopgun.com) for you to download as a guide.

Here then (Table 32) is my analogous set of checklists for our purposes:

TABLE 32 - CHECKLISTS Я US

Aviation	TILT
Walkaround	Make it Purposeful
Pre-Start	Make it Personal

Aviation	TILT
Taxi	Make if Emotional
Takeoff	Make it Compelling
Climb	Make it Visual
Cruise	Make a Request
Descent	Prepare
Landing	Deliver
Shutdown	Debrief

I will use the supplemental boxes as follows:

- **WARNING:** Failure to follow could harm your career.
- **CAUTION:** Failure to follow could harm your listener(s) (e.g., eye fatigue, bladder leaks, boredom).
- **Note:** An essential tip never to be shared with Air Force vets.

A ROSE BY ANY OTHER NAME

One of the core storyline elements of both *Top Gun* movies were the call signs. Maverick, the "independent individual who doesn't go along with a group or party."[96]

Iceman: cool under pressure.

Viper: he'll sting you when you're not looking.

Goose: someone who's silly, cracking jokes all the time.

Normally, call signs are assigned to you by your squadron mates based on an unimaginatively appropriate conjunction of your last name or, like Maverick, Goose, and Viper, an interpretation of the way you behave, or, most embarrassingly, an incident you'd rather forget—the adult form of fraternal bullying. Here are some real examples, some more colorful than

96 https://www.merriam-webster.com/dictionary/maverick

others, that I think you'll enjoy as my way of orchestrating your mood away from the neuron frying heavy academics in this book towards something lighter yet equally memorable because of the context.

The first two examples are rated "adult content only," so skip the next paragraph if you must, because you'll never be able to unread them.

Long before the Russian performance art group Pussy Riot, there was "Pussy" Galore from the movie Goldfinger (no, I don't benefit from any royalties). One could reasonably argue that that call sign would likely not be acceptable in our current Navy culture. Well, in 1992–1993, the world-famous Blue Angels, the Navy's flight demonstration squadron, had a Lieutenant Larry Packer with the equally vulgar call sign: "Fudge." When I first arrived at NAS Miramar, I rented a room in a large house with a few other bachelor aviators including then Lieutenant Dennis Bates. Call sign … wait for it … "Master" … of course.

More G-rated call signs included Steve "Skaggs" Bos, or legend of all legends, John "Bug" Roach, and Tom "Booty" Boutin (a squadron mate of mine who can be seen on the carrier flight deck in the opening scenes of the first movie). When you have a few moments, do a web search on Bug and you'll see why he's a legend, most famously for his talkdown of an A-6 Intruder with landing gear problems that had to perform a net recovery (instead of a wire trap) … at night … on a pitching deck … in the stormy, cold waters near Alaska.

Classically, just about every squadron had that one guy that was constantly pursuing all manner of women, in every port, drunk or sober, earning him the nickname "Hound," as in bloodhound. Warning: don't ever marry a flyboy with the nickname Hound. Or the guy that's known for always borrowing money, "Mooch."

On the ignominious side, there's the case of the F-14 pilot that showed up for his first operational squadron tour (VF-111) insisting his callsign was "Shark" only for the moniker "Minnow" to be properly bestowed on him at the official squadron-naming ceremony. Or the time on my second deployment, when there were two F-14 crewmen that had snuck liquor aboard and stashed it in their stateroom (their sleeping quarters). One night, "Hulk" (if you saw his size, you'd know how he got the callsign) became an aggressive drunk and flung his small stateroom refrigerator at his whiskey wingman, cutting open the bridge of his nose down to the cartilage. New callsign: "Fridge." Or the time one of my VAW-114 squadron mates was walking on the flight deck at night without paying attention, fell through an open hatch breaking his arm when he landed ten feet below—the plaster cast meant keeping him off the flight schedule for weeks. Callsign: "Hatch."

Finally, and most humorously, one of two anti-social lieutenants in my squadron decided it was a good idea to burn some classified material in his stateroom instead of walking a few minutes to the Ready Room to destroy the documents in the approved cross-cut shredder. With smoke wafting out of his door, a passerby triggered a call to the Bridge initiating a "General Quarters" announcement for the on-duty firefighting party to rush to the scene of the smoke. Dressed to the nines in all their firefighting regalia and armed with a high-pressure hose of unlimited sea water, they busted into his stateroom to see him hunched over a round metal trashcan innocently throwing pieces of paper into the small campfire. Callsign? You guessed it, "Torch."

Naturally, medical officers and dentists universally get "Doc" assigned as their callsign. Once, while visiting me on my fourth ship and being introduced to our ship's dentist, my then nine-year-old daughter asked, "Why don't you call him Dent?" Thus began a whole new tradition.

Anyway, back to my BFF Dave for a moment. Plain 'ol Doc wasn't good enough. As a flight surgeon, he was required to log a certain number of flight hours annually to maintain his flight status (and supplemental flight pay). As the airwing flight surgeon, he was able to ride on every multi-seat platform in our wing, from Tomcat to Hawkeye. On his very first flight in an F-14, he was given a safety brief to ride in the backseat and some rudimentary guidance on how to get the radar turned on and operating properly.

We were in the middle of the ocean during our '86–'87 deployment on the USS CARL VINSON (CVN-70), with no expectations of any Soviet surveillance aircraft in our vicinity. Doc and his pilot were launched as the "wingman" Tomcat on a training mission to turn jet fuel into noise. Low and behold, intelligence reports a Soviet Tu-95 Bear inbound to the carrier and the flight of two Tomcats, with Doc in the backseat of the trailing aircraft, are vectored to intercept. Then, the lead aircraft reports a system problem. His radar is Tango Uniform, military slang for his radar system being dead, lying "tits up," as the saying goes. By protocol, Doc's pilot must take over as the lead plane and, while flying towards the Bear, simultaneously tries talking Doc through the necessary steps to get the tracking radar to lock onto the target. He was laughingly unsuccessful so a new callsign was immediately bestowed upon landing … "No Lock Doc."

So how did I get the blatantly obvious, entirely unimaginative Goldy moniker?

I reported to my first operational squadron in 1984 as the only officer that had been commissioned through the ROTC program. Everyone else was either a Naval Academy graduate or commissioned through the Aviation Officer Candidate (AOC) program. Some of you may recall the movie Animal House, the most profitable comedy in history (a near 50x return on a mere $3 million budget) which had come out just a few years prior. In that movie there was an over-the-top ROTC Cadet Commander named Neidermeyer. That's what they tried to pin on me. Fortunately, the number of characters using the regulation font exceeded the allowable length on my flight suit nametag. In exasperation, somebody said, "Oh, crap, just call him Goldy."

Phew, dodged a bullet.

WTF, OVER?

The day before I graduated from college, we had our official Navy commissioning ceremony where I was awarded the Naval Institute Leadership Award for my role as the Drill Team Commander. The award came with a little plaque and a copy of DICNAVAB—the aptly named *Dictionary of Naval Abbreviations*. As you likely know already, the military in general and aviation in particular have a ton of linguistic distinctions—that's a fancy way of saying "jargon." For your infotainment, Table 33 contains a few "brevity codes" (that's jargon for our jargon) that you might find useful the next time you go to the theater (does anyone go to the theater anymore?):

Table 33 — "You talkin' to me?!"

Brevity Code	Meaning	Usage
99	Message intended for all entities on the radio circuit.	Controller: "99 aircraft, report fuel states in order."
Alpha Strike	Large group of multiple aircraft types whose mission is to strike a critical enemy target.	Captain on the ship's intercom: "Attention all hands. We're launching a 30-plane Alpha Strike in two hours. This is the real thing, so I want everybody to focus on the task at hand and get everyone back safely."
Angels	Altitude in thousands of feet.	Controller: "Ghostrider 203, take Angels 10."
Bogey	Radar or visual contact of an unidentified aircraft.	Controller: "Ghostrider, vector 090 for Bogey, 40 miles."
Bandit	Contact identified as an enemy aircraft.	Controller: "Your Bandit, 3 O'clock, 5 miles."
BDA	Battle Damage Assessment made either by direct observation of the bombs' impact or gleaned after the fact from intelligence analysis.	Phoenix: "Dagger 3 is mission complete. Unable BDA due to low clouds."
Bingo	Enough fuel to return to base (RTB)	Goose: "Ghostrider 203 is bingo, RTB."
Bravo Zulu	Congratulations on your accomplishment.	Controller: "BDA on the target looks good. CAG passes a BZ to the Strike Package.
Bullseye	A battlefield reference point.	Controller: "Your target, 8 miles west of Bullseye."
CAG	Airwing Commander (holdover from older days when it stood for Commander of the Air Group).	Squadron Duty Officer: "Maverick and Goose, CAG wants to see you in his office, ASAP!"

Brevity Code	Meaning	Usage
Copy	I heard you and wrote down the essentials.	Controller: "Dagger flight, there'll be a tanker overhead mother, callsign Bucket 104." Dagger Lead: "Copy."
Feet Dry	Crossing the boundary from sea to land.	Maverick: "Dagger flight is Feet Dry."
Feet Wet	Returning from an overland mission when crossing from land to sea.	Phoenix: "Dagger 3 is Feet Wet."
FNG	Fucking new guy or gal. Squadron rookie.	Squadron Duty Officer: "Hey FNG, your turn to make the coffee."
Fox (x)	1 – Fired a semi-active radar missile. 2 – Fired a heat seeking missile. 3 – Fired an active radar missile.	(From Independence Day) "Eagle 1, Fox 3." "Eagle 20, Fox 2."
Gadget	Radar	"My gadget is tango uniform." (See Tango Uniform)
Knock it Off	Stop whatever you're doing. (usually only used during a training mission)	"99, knock it off for range safety issue."
No Joy	Unable to visually acquire the target.	"In the clouds, no joy on my wingman."
Out* or Out here	Signing off a radio circuit or phone call.	Cdr. Lovell: "Houston, we're at stable 1, the ship is secure. This is Apollo 13. Out here."
Over*	I've finished talking, it's now your turn. Usually only used on circuits with a lot of static or background noise making it difficult to know when the other party has finished.	Cdr. Lovell: "Houston. Did I hear you right? You want us to shut down the fuel cells. Over."

Brevity Code	Meaning	Usage
Roger*	I understand what you just said.	Mission Control: "Apollo, Houston. You have about 15 minutes of power left in the Command Module." Cdr. Lovell: "Roger, Houston."
RTB	Return to Base.	Controller: "Ghostrider 203, your signal is RTB."
Sierra Hotel	That was a shit hot thing you just did.	Goose: "Mav, that was a Sierra Hotel flyby of the tower."
Tally Ho	Visual contact has been made.	"Tally Ho on the Bogey at 2 miles. Investigating."
TTP	Tactics, Techniques, and Procedures. Our rules to live (or die) by.	"Maverick seems to be rewriting the TTPs for this attack plan."
Tango Uniform	My system is dead, as in, it's like a body lying tits up on the floor.	"My gadget is tango uniform."
Wilco*	I will comply with your request/order.	Controller: "Maverick, take angels 12." Maverick: "Wilco."
WTF, over	What the fuck was that? Explain yourself.	Tower Controller immediately following the unsanctioned high- speed flyby: "Ghostrider, WTF, over!!!"

*Only one of these words can ever be uttered at one time on the radio. Like John Wick violating the Continental hotel's rules under threat of incommunicado, ***don't ever, ever, ever say:*** "Roger, wilco, over and out." (I got scared just typing that!)

This completes your Boot Camp introduction to Naval aviation. You're ready to launch into your first presentation planning mission.

BEST OF THE BEST

Instead of a checklist to follow Step 8, what I encourage you to do now is to take the murder board review form (Table 31) and practice using it on some real-world presentations. Pick a handful of online presentations or read some transcripts of topics you're interested in. The subject matter and length are not as important as the skill you need to develop as a reviewer.

I have selected three specific speeches that demonstrate nearly all the TTPs I've written about, starting with President Kennedy's Moon Speech in third place.

KENNEDY'S MOON SPEECH

In the late 1950s, with the launch of Sputnik 1 by the Union of Soviet Socialist Republics (USSR), the United States and the USSR embarked on what is now referred to as the Space Race. In May of 1961, then President John F. Kennedy famously declared, in a speech to the US Congress, that the US would land a man on the moon within the decade (he was not yet inclusive enough to include the option of it being a woman). One year later, almost a century after Lincoln (99 years to be precise), Kennedy gave a clarifying speech at Rice University Stadium in Houston, Texas, near where the future Johnson Space Center was under construction.

Here is that speech:

> President Pitzer, Mr. Vice President, Governor, Congressman Thomas, Senator Wiley, and Congressman Miller, Mr. Webb, Mr. Bell, scientists, distinguished guests, and ladies and gentlemen:
>
> I appreciate your president having made me an honorary visiting professor, and I will assure you that my first lecture will be very brief.

[Squirt of dopamine in anticipation of a short presentation.]

> I am delighted to be here and I'm particularly delighted to be here on this occasion.
>
> We meet at a college noted for knowledge, in a city noted for progress, in a State noted for strength, and we stand in need

of all three, for we meet in an hour of change and challenge, in a decade of hope and fear, in an age of both knowledge and ignorance. The greater our knowledge increases, the greater our ignorance unfolds.

[Notice how he immediately DOSEs the audience with both dopamine and oxytocin when complementing the college, the city, and the state. Also notice the somewhat musical rhythm of that last paragraph - "college noted for knowledge, city noted for progress ... " Lovely to read and listen to.]

Despite the striking fact that most of the scientists that the world has ever known are alive and working today, despite the fact that this Nation's own scientific manpower is doubling every twelve years in a rate of growth more than three times that of our population as a whole, despite that, the vast stretches of the unknown and the unanswered and the unfinished still far outstrip our collective comprehension.

[Just a smidgen of epinephrine (fear chemical) about how much we don't know about our world.]

No man can fully grasp how far and how fast we have come, but condense, if you will, the 50,000 years of man's recorded history in a time span of but a half a century. Stated in these terms, we know very little about the first forty years, except at the end of them advanced man had learned to use the skins of animals to cover them. Then about ten years ago, under this standard, man emerged from his caves to construct other kinds of shelter. Only five years ago man learned to write and use a cart with wheels. Christianity began less than two years ago. The printing press came this year, and then less than two months ago, during this whole fifty-year span of human history, the steam engine provided a new source of power.

Newton explored the meaning of gravity. Last month electric lights and telephones and automobiles and airplanes became available. Only last week did we develop penicillin and television and nuclear power, and now if America's new spacecraft succeeds in reaching Venus, we will have literally reached the stars before midnight tonight.

[This starts Freytag's Pyramid with Exposition of the narrative—e.g., the last 50,000 years of modern human history.]

> This is a breathtaking pace, and such a pace cannot help but create new ills as it dispels old, new ignorance, new problems, new dangers. Surely the opening vistas of space promise high costs and hardships, as well as high reward.

[This is the Conflict of the story. We know a lot but there's a lot more to learn and we were really surprised when the Soviets launched a satellite before us. Continues his DOSEing by explaining both the fear ("high costs and hardships") and the reward ahead.]

> So, it is not surprising that some would have us stay where we are a little longer to rest, to wait. But this city of Houston, this State of Texas, this country of the United States was not built by those who waited and rested and wished to look behind them. This country was conquered by those who moved forward—and so will space.
>
> William Bradford, speaking in 1630 of the founding of the Plymouth Bay Colony, said that all great and honorable actions are accompanied with great difficulties, and both must be enterprised and overcome with answerable courage.

[A little more epinephrine.]

> If this capsule history of our progress teaches us anything, it is that man, in his quest for knowledge and progress, is determined and cannot be deterred. The exploration of space will go ahead, whether we join in it or not, and it is one of the great adventures of all time, and no nation which expects to be the leader of other nations can expect to stay behind in the race for space.
>
> Those who came before us made certain that this country rode the first waves of the industrial revolutions, the first waves of modern invention, and the first wave of nuclear power, and this generation does not intend to founder in the backwash of the coming age of space. We mean to be a part of it--we mean to lead it. For the eyes of the world now look into space, to the

> moon and to the planets beyond, and we have vowed that we shall not see it governed by a hostile flag of conquest, but by a banner of freedom and peace. We have vowed that we shall not see space filled with weapons of mass destruction, but with instruments of knowledge and understanding.

[Dopamine]

> Yet the vows of this Nation can only be fulfilled if we in this Nation are first, and, therefore, we intend to be first. In short, our leadership in science and in industry, our hopes for peace and security, our obligations to ourselves as well as others, all require us to make this effort, to solve these mysteries, to solve them for the good of all men, and to become the world's leading space-faring nation.

[There's some masterful mood management in these past few paragraphs as he starts to shift everyone's anxiousness and skepticism about the Soviet space program towards a mood of resolution and ambition.]

> We set sail on this new sea because there is new knowledge to be gained, and new rights to be won, and they must be won and used for the progress of all people. For space science, like nuclear science and all technology, has no conscience of its own. Whether it will become a force for good or ill depends on man, and only if the United States occupies a position of pre-eminence can we help decide whether this new ocean will be a sea of peace or a new terrifying theater of war. I do not say that we should or will go unprotected against the hostile misuse of space any more than we go unprotected against the hostile use of land or sea, but I do say that space can be explored and mastered without feeding the fires of war, without repeating the mistakes that man has made in extending his writ around this globe of ours.

[In a non-linear fashion (like the movie Pulp Fiction), he's already starting to lay out the Denouement, the end of this moon-shot rainbow.]

> There is no strife, no prejudice, no national conflict in outer space as yet. Its hazards are hostile to us all. Its conquest

deserves the best of all mankind, and its opportunity for peaceful cooperation may never come again. But why, some say, the moon? Why choose this as our goal? And they may well ask why climb the highest mountain? Why, 35 years ago, fly the Atlantic? Why does Rice play Texas?

[That last sentence is just brilliant. Texans live and die by football and the Rice Owls versus the University of Texas Longhorns was a fearsome rivalry. If you watch a recording of the speech, you'll see that those last five words led to a rousing uproar from the crowd, producing a massive DOSE of oxytocin. It was also a quite funny interjection, but not humor for humor's sake. It was to setup and to reinforce the point he would make in the next paragraph about the American preference for hard challenges.]

We choose to go to the moon. We choose to go to the moon in this decade and do the other things, not because they are easy, but because they are hard, because that goal will serve to organize and measure the best of our energies and skills, because that challenge is one that we are willing to accept, one we are unwilling to postpone, and one which we intend to win, and the others, too.

It is for these reasons that I regard the decision last year to shift our efforts in space from low to high gear as among the most important decisions that will be made during my incumbency in the office of the Presidency.

[This is the Initiating Event of the pyramid.]

In the last 24 hours we have seen facilities now being created for the greatest and most complex exploration in man's history. We have felt the ground shake and the air shattered by the testing of a Saturn C-1 booster rocket, many times as powerful as the Atlas which launched John Glenn, generating power equivalent to 10,000 automobiles with their accelerators on the floor. We have seen the site where five F-1 rocket engines, each one as powerful as all eight engines of the Saturn combined, will be clustered together to make the advanced Saturn missile, assembled in a new building to be built at Cape Canaveral as tall as a 48-story structure, as wide as a city block, and as long as two lengths of this field.

Within these last nineteen months at least 45 satellites have circled the earth. Some forty of them were "made in the United States of America" and they were far more sophisticated and supplied far more knowledge to the people of the world than those of the Soviet Union.

The Mariner spacecraft, now on its way to Venus, is the most intricate instrument in the history of space science. The accuracy of that shot is comparable to firing a missile from Cape Canaveral and dropping it in this stadium between the forty-yard lines.

Transit satellites are helping our ships at sea to steer a safer course. Tiros satellites have given us unprecedented warnings of hurricanes and storms, and will do the same for forest fires and icebergs.

[Four paragraphs of Rising Action.]

We have had our failures, but so have others, even if they do not admit them. And they may be less public.

To be sure, we are behind, and will be behind for some time in manned flight. But we do not intend to stay behind, and in this decade, we shall make up and move ahead.

The growth of our science and education will be enriched by new knowledge of our universe and environment, by new techniques of learning and mapping and observation, by new tools and computers for industry, medicine, the home as well as the school. Technical institutions, such as Rice, will reap the harvest of these gains.

And finally, the space effort itself, while still in its infancy, has already created a great number of new companies, and tens of thousands of new jobs. Space and related industries are generating new demands in investment and skilled personnel, and this city and this State, and this region, will share greatly in this growth. What was once the furthest outpost on the old frontier of the West will be the furthest outpost on the new frontier of science and space. Houston, your City of Houston, with its Manned Spacecraft Center, will become the heart of a large scientific and engineering community. During the next 5 years the National Aeronautics and Space Administration expects to double the number of scientists and engineers in this area, to increase its outlays for salaries and expenses to $60 million a year; to invest some $200 million in plant and laboratory facilities; and to direct or contract for new space efforts over $1 billion from this Center in this City.

[Four paragraphs of falling action.]

To be sure, all this costs us all a good deal of money. This year's space budget is three times what it was in January 1961, and it is greater than the space budget of the previous eight years combined. That budget now stands at $5,400 million a year—a staggering sum, though somewhat less than we pay for cigarettes and cigars every year. Space expenditures will soon rise some more, from 40 cents per person per week to more than 50 cents a week for every man, woman and child in the United Stated, for we have given this program a high national priority--even though I realize that this is in some measure an act of faith and vision, for we do not now know what benefits await us. But if I were to say, my fellow citizens, that we shall send to the moon, 240,000 miles away from the control station in Houston, a giant rocket more than 300 feet tall, the length of this football field, made of new metal alloys, some of which have not yet been invented, capable of standing heat and stresses several times more than have ever been experienced, fitted together with a precision better than the finest watch, carrying all the equipment needed for propulsion, guidance, control, communications, food and survival, on an untried mission, to an unknown celestial body, and then return it safely to earth, re-entering the atmosphere at speeds of over 25,000 miles per hour, causing heat about half that of the temperature of the sun--almost as hot as it is here today--and do all this, and do it right, and do it first before this decade is out--then we must be bold.

[Almost done, so now is the time to Make his Request—support his administration's budget for this effort.]

> I'm the one who is doing all the work, so we just want you to stay cool for a minute. [laughter]

[Note: Not a prepared remark. He needed to pause to wipe the sweat from his forehead.]

> However, I think we're going to do it, and I think that we must pay what needs to be paid. I don't think we ought to waste any money, but I think we ought to do the job. And this will be done in the decade of the sixties. It may be done while some of you are still here at school at this college and university. It will be done during the term of office of some of the people who sit here on this platform. But it will be done. And it will be done before the end of this decade.

> I am delighted that this university is playing a part in putting a man on the moon as part of a great national effort of the United States of America.

[More oxytocin.]

> Many years ago, the great British explorer George Mallory, who was to die on Mount Everest, was asked why he wanted to climb it. He said, "Because it is there."

> Well, space is there, and we're going to climb it, and the moon and the planets are there, and new hopes for knowledge and peace are there. And, therefore, as we set sail we ask God's blessing on the most hazardous and dangerous and greatest adventure on which man has ever embarked.

[Reminding the audience of the Resolution and Denouement.]

> Thank you.

To summarize, the true purpose of this presentation was to get the American citizenry onboard with his plan. He's asking for their hard-earned tax dollars to pay for this effort. He's asking for a national effort from engineers, scientists, universities, technicians, etc., to get involved. And lastly, quite boldly, he's asking his faith leader to not let him down.

I'd encourage you to watch the speech at least twice so that you can notice the brilliance yourself. It's about the length of a TED Talk, so he lived up to his promise to "make his first lecture very brief," comparing it to a university professor's typical hour-long lecture.

You should be able to find it at the JFK Library's website here:

https://www.jfklibrary.org/learn/about-jfk/historic-speeches/address-at-rice-university-on-the-nations-space-effort_

Although President Kennedy was a former naval officer, it is unlikely that he crafted that speech on his own. Therefore, my congratulations are extended to his speech writing staff as well. Yet another TTP I would encourage for a truly consequential talk—get help from others. Especially others who have read this book or attended my workshop.

This may sound self-serving, but I liken it to another high-consequence situation. In a hospital operating room, you'll find a surgeon, a surgical nurse, and an anesthetist. Three individuals with entirely different educational backgrounds yet in that room they share a set of distinctions that allow them to work together more effectively and efficiently. For that same reason, practice "operating" with colleagues who share the TTPs from this program.

LINCOLN'S GETTYSBURG ADDRESS

In second place is President Abraham Lincoln's Gettysburg Address. Written more than a century before TOPGUN was a gleam in a couple of fighter pilots' sierra hotel sunglasses, it has been reported that he wrote the speech himself (as he was known to do with all his written works[97]) while riding on the train up from Washington.

By way of historical background (e.g., the Exposition of the story), during the 19th century Civil War in the United States, over 175,000 men fought the fiercest of battles in the rolling hills of Pennsylvania. While the Battle of Gettysburg lasted a mere three days, nearly one third of all

97 https://www.smithsonianmag.com/history/ted-sorensen-on-abraham-lincoln-a-man-of-his-words-12048177/

those involved were either killed, wounded, captured, or missing. It was the deadliest battle of the war and produced the largest loss of general officers.

Five months later, on November 19, 1863, during the dedication of the Soldier's National Cemetery in Gettysburg, Abraham Lincoln delivered a short but long-remembered speech. Unlike Kennedy's speech, I'll not interrupt the flow with my commentary, which follows the speech.

> Four score and seven years ago our fathers brought forth on this continent, a new nation, conceived in Liberty, and dedicated to the proposition that all men are created equal.
>
> Now we are engaged in a great civil war, testing whether that nation, or any nation so conceived and so dedicated, can long endure. We are met on a great battlefield of that war. We have come to dedicate a portion of that field, as a final resting place for those who here gave their lives that that nation might live. It is altogether fitting and proper that we should do this.
>
> But, in a larger sense, we cannot dedicate—we cannot consecrate—we cannot hallow—this ground. The brave men, living and dead, who struggled here, have consecrated it, far above our poor power to add or detract. The world will little note, nor long remember what we say here, but it can never forget what they did here. It is for us the living, rather, to be dedicated here to the unfinished work which they who fought here have thus far so nobly advanced. It is rather for us to be here dedicated to the great task remaining before us—that from these honored dead we take increased devotion to that cause for which they gave the last full measure of devotion—that we here highly resolve that these dead shall not have died in vain—that this nation, under God, shall have a new birth of freedom—and that government of the people, by the people, for the people, shall not perish from the earth."

"The world will little note, nor long remember" my ass. This talk contains such a powerful message that it is carved into the granite walls of the Lincoln Memorial in D.C., seen by many millions.

STEP 1: MAKE IT PURPOSEFUL

Lincoln's purpose was two-fold. First, he wanted to help heal the nation after the extraordinary loss of life. Second, he wanted to steel the resolve of the remaining Union Army soldiers to continue fighting towards victory: "… to be here dedicated to the great task remaining before us …"

STEP 2: MAKE IT PERSONAL

In a speech of only 268 words, he used the collective pronouns "we," "us," and "our" fifteen times.

STEP 3: MAKE IT EMOTIONAL

Immediately before Lincoln, the Honorable Edward Everett, former Congressman, Senator, and Secretary of State, delivered his talk. At age 69, Everett had earned a reputation as a great orator. He gave a two-hour speech, a common occurrence for cemetery dedications at the time, that almost nobody is aware of (except you now).

Lincoln's speech lasted a mere two minutes yet struck such an emotional chord that it is now etched in granite for hundreds of thousands of annual visitors to view and reflect.

STEP 4: MAKE IT COMPELLING

The narrative follows Freytag's Pyramid with precision as depicted in Figure 25.

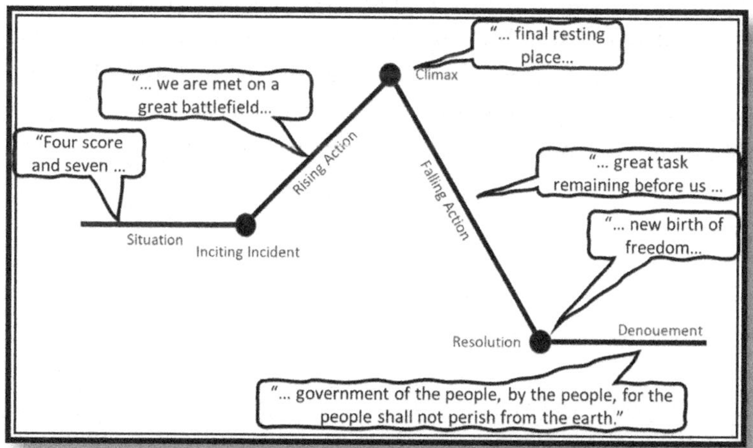

FIGURE 25 — EVEN LINCOLN KNEW NARRATIVE NAVIGATION

STEP 5: MAKE IT VISUAL

I've been to the Gettysburg Memorial. The site of all those names on all those statues is overwhelming. I can only imagine how visceral the visual backdrop was to this speech mere months after the horrific battle, perhaps with military equipment still strewn about in various states of battle damage and disrepair.

Not to take anything away from Kennedy's Moon Speech, but imagine how much greater the impact might have been had he been on or near the then existing launch pad in Florida. So why then at Rice University? Because, as he said, it's located in the heart of Houston, Texas, the site of NASA's headquarters. Okay, I guess he did manage the visual scene appropriately.

STEP 6: MAKE A REQUEST

Lincoln made one very simple but profoundly moving request, more of a demand actually, aligned with his purpose:

"... highly resolve that these dead shall not have died in vain..."

A mood shift for sure!

IPHONE LAUNCH

Of the hundreds, perhaps thousands, of presentations I've watched over the years, none displays the full gamut of TTPs that I have discussed in this book better than the 1st Place winner, Steve Jobs' launch of the iPhone on January 9, 2007, for MacWorld. I encourage you to do a web search for the full-length video and watch it once by yourself to see if you can spot some of the TTPs (e.g. Trust Their EARS, Us versus Them, A ROAD to Action). Then, refer to my analysis in Table 34 below, not as an answer sheet, per se, but rather as my top picks for some of the clearest examples.

TABLE 34 - DIAGNOSING THE SUPREME SALESMAN

Time Stamp	TTP	What I noticed
N/A	Scenario & Purpose	"Inform the Industry" MacWorld is an annual event for Apple aficionados. His purpose was to spread a wide net of Prospects. This was in January, but the product didn't ship until June.
0:00-0:07	Prepare the Listener	Deliberately walks across the stage in silence. Builds anticipation.
0:07-0:18	Make it Personal	"I've been looking forward to this for two and a half years." And many in the audience know what's coming so it's emotional for them as well.
0:51-0:24	Trust Their EARS & Us	Review of the Macintosh and the iPod reminds everyone of their past engagement, ability, reliability, and sincerity (EARS). It also reminds everyone in the room that MacWorld is an Us congregation.
0:27-2:15	DOSEing	Notice how he elicits dopamine-fueled clapping with each of the three product intros. Also notice how the applause on the 3rd was much more subdued. If I could've made one recommendation to him, I would've started with the 3rd and finished with the mobile phone to create a crescendo of applause. But who am I to tell Steve how to do his job?!
2:55	Mood Orchestration	He absolutely kills it here when he explains how all three are rolled up into one. The mood of the entire room was already high on curiosity, and he takes it to the next level which a shift to resolution and ambition ("I gotta get me one").

Time Stamp	TTP	What I noticed
3:17	Humor	Notice the humorous image is directly relevant to his product launch. He's making fun of traditional phone manufacturers while being playful.
3:40-4:30	Freytag's Pyramid	He sets out the exposition, the current situation of cell phones, and the existing conflict—e.g.,, smart phones that aren't so smart.
4:50	Hands Free	Notice how he walks over to the side, takes a sip of water, then returns to the presentation. He does not walk around with the bottle in hand.
4:50-15:00	Pyramid-Rising Action	He starts the rising action with the user interface. He continues the rising action with a description of the operating system, proximity sensor, light sensor, etc.
15:30-16:50	Pyramid-Climax	He's demonstrating a finished product, live, with the audience fully engaged.
16:50	DOSE-Oxytocin	Do you think he picked "With a little help from my friends" accidentally? Brilliant manipulation of oxytocin.
50:50	SPIE & LEFT	Jobs had to SPIE on Schmidt to develop the working relationship. Having Schmidt on the Apple Board of Directors also helped him to understand his LEFT.
52:33	SPIE-company culture	Schmidt: "The cultures are similar." SPIEing works at a corporate level too. It's possible to understand corporate Identity and look for a match (or mismatch in the case of Apple's famous 1984 Super Bowl ad for the Macintosh).

Time Stamp	TTP	What I noticed
1:04:40-1:08:30	Pyramid-Falling Action	Answers the questions: How much? Where can I get one?
1:09:30-1:14:18	Not-Prepared, Not-emotional, Not-visual, No-DOSEing	Notice how the Cingular/AT&T CEO had to refer to his notes on index cards. Notice how little emotionality he infuses into his part of the talk. There was nothing inspiring in his words. He said he was excited, but it came off as a bit stiff and insincere to me. Notice the mood shift you yourself experienced while listening to him.
1:15:03-1:16:14	We just make shit up	I love that when his clicker breaks down, he just launches into an unscripted, humorous anecdote from his early years with Woz. The humor is both real and relevant, and keeps the audience engaged instead of being distracted by the breakdown. Again, friggin' brilliant!
1:16:15-1:17:05	Resolution	He resolved to capture 1% of the mobile phone market by 2008.
1:17:05-1:17:18	Make a Request	"This is a very competitive market." This statement is another way of saying, "Hey, for us to reach 1%, we need your help. Please support our ambition to reach 1% by buying one yourself and telling your friends to do the same."
1:17:30-1:18:00	Denouement	Renaming the computer to Apple Inc. (by dropping "computer") implies a long-term vision to offer other products that have nothing to do with computers. Like iWatch, and Airpods, which came years later. Amazing foresight.

Time Stamp	TTP	What I noticed
1:18:08-1:19:10	Make a Request	This is an implied 2nd request as he finishes the talk. He reminds everyone about the Wayne Gretzky quote, and is basically saying to the crowd: "Please help us stay ahead of the puck."

Some additional observations that apply more globally:

- Maximum use of graphics and minimal use of text
- Each slide is crisp and clean with zero excess content
- Notice how well-rehearsed this was without being memorized

Outcome: As it turns out, they captured their 1% market share goal by the Fall of 2007 and by the end of 2008 had reached a staggering 10.7%[98] —roughly 100 million units.

98 https://www.statista.com/statistics/216459/global-market-share-of-apple-iphone/

DAVE BROWN EULOGY

DAVE BROWN
RENAISSANCE MAN

My name is Jeff Goldfinger – the "Goldy" you may have heard mention of. I first met Dave in the Officer's Club in September of 1985. He had just reported to Naval Aviation's Carrier Airwing Fifteen as a flight surgeon. I was riding around in the back of E-2 Hawkeyes as an air controller back then.

For those of you that don't know anything about flight surgeons, besides your commanding officer, they're the most feared individuals in all military aviation. A flight surgeon has this magical power to see right through our lies and deceit and find that blocked sinus or fluid filled lung or overstressed psyche and then the jig is up. We have been discovered. We're grounded!

So that's how we met. I walked straight up to him, like the cowardly lion in his first encounter with Dorothy, and started talking to him. And for those of you who know me well, I've been talking ever since. And just like Dorothy, Dave immediately took pity on me, and that was the start of an eighteen-year friendship.

We spent the next three years together in San Diego. We were housemates for part of that time, and he would frequently cry on my shoulder about his current career crisis. He was doing the doctor thing back then, performing dozens upon dozens of physicals on some of the healthiest individuals this country can produce, and I must tell you that he was a bit frustrated by the monotony of it all. He was questioning whether "physician" was his true calling.

But one day he came home from work, bounded through the front door, delightfully animated. So, I asked him "What's goin' on?"

"Goldy!" he shouted with pride. "I got to resuscitate my first full cardiac arrest!"

I guess you have to be a doctor to understand.

Fast forward a couple of years and Dave and I find ourselves in Fallon, Nevada, together—a town where the humidity is measured in single digits and a night on the town is something called "Pigs in Space." The carrier guys know what I'm talkin' about. In San Diego, I used to spot him when he was learning to fly a hang glider. Here we are, years later, and we're dropping bombs together from an A-6 down at Nellis.

Let me say that again: Doctor Dave and Goldy the air controller are dropping ordnance from a Navy jet flying over an Air Force bombing range while a guy on the ground is designating the target with a laser spot. You have to be a military aviator to understand the irony of all that.

From Fallon, we were both sent to Naval Air Station Pax River, Maryland, for different reasons but where a year later he was selected for the astronaut program. To sum it up, Dave went from hang gliding to shuttle flying, and throughout it all he allowed me to live vicariously through him. I was there at the bottom of the hill as he glided down from the top of Black Mountain in San Diego. And I was there in the bleachers at the Cape on February 1st as he glided down from the top of the atmosphere. But unlike that day in San Diego, I wasn't able to tell him how great a landing he had just made. So, I'm grateful to Dave's family for allowing me the opportunity to honor Dave by sharing a few thoughts with you today.

As many of you know, Dave sent out a final email the day before the scheduled landing. It was the most magnificent compilation of his sixteen-day experience, but more importantly it expressed a hope for a peaceful future. The email was sent to a few dozen addressees—obviously an arbitrary limitation imposed by the shuttle's computer system because as you can see from the turnout here today, he would have sent it to each and every one of you if he had had the chance.

Anyway, that email started the most wonderfully therapeutic chain of emails from all the people he touched over the years, from all walks of life, from a wide variety of academic, social, and economic circles—many of whom are in this audience today. So, with your collective permission, I'd like to share some snippets from those emails because they will forever cement the image we all have of this "Renaissance Man" that we call Dave Brown.

Let me start by paraphrasing Doug T.'s letter: "Many of the other pilots like to say that after Doc got his pilot's wings, he forgot that he was also a flight doc. It was said that if you had a broken leg, Doc would tell you to take two aspirins and don't call him in the morning 'cause he'd be out flying."

Here's another memory. "He approached his training with an awareness and appreciation of the difficulty and the risks involved yet always with a smile and sense of enjoyment, even glee." You would think that statement was written by Jack N., one of his NASA instructors and dearest friends, or maybe Jay S., one of his Navy instructors. But it was really written by Heidi M., a fellow gymnast, talking about Dave's early days in the Circus Kingdom.

Debby R. wrote: "When I got divorced Dave sent me a very caring letter that I carried around with me for a long time in my purse. It helped tremendously because I knew someone cared." I'm here to tell you that he wasn't just a good listener to Debby. He was like that to everyone, but especially to me. As 51% of the human population will tell you, men have a hard time talking openly and honestly with women, much less other men. Well, Dave was one of my sounding boards and, like Debby, I will miss him dearly.

So, what was Dave like to some of the others out there? He was a fellow medical student to Gordon, a gymnast to Heidi, a unicyclist to Trudy and Dave H., a juggler to Jessica

H., a clown to Robert M., an intern to Jane B., a doctor to "Dragon" Bien, a flight surgeon to Airwing Fifteen, a dual designator to Bud L., a biker to Zip and Nancy, a tail dragger to Al, and "Astronomer Dave" to Noel R.

Let me tell you a little bit more about Noel. A few years ago, Ms. Laura F., a Hartford, Connecticut teacher in the Polaris Day Program for special needs kids, was starting a lesson plan on astronomy and asked her sister Gloria if Dave could send a signed picture or something similarly insignificant to an astronaut but immensely valuable to Laura's kids. Well, a picture just wasn't enough for Dave. He had to get involved. So, in classic Dave fashion, he contacted Laura and asked her how he could help. And from that austere beginning evolved a friendship between two budding astronomers.

"Astronomer Noel" is here with us today, getting ready to graduate from high school—an accomplishment that even he will tell you seemed out of reach just a few short years ago. Dave understood that the future of this great country of ours lies squarely in the laps of all the Noels out there. So, I say to you Noel, look around. Even though Dave may no longer be here to help you, don't hesitate to call upon this room full of his friends if you ever need anything.

This was the measure of Dave's character. It was never about him but always about the other person. Never once did he ask for attention or recognition or glory. He was the humblest overachiever we have ever known.

Well, today it's about you, Dave. All of this. For you. Our Renaissance Man who was a lecturer to Fields R., a digital photographer to Triple, a filmmaker to his Columbia crewmates, a storyteller to Bestor C., a listener to Debby, "Uncle" Dave to my daughters Jami and Jacey, and a President to his colleagues in the International Association of Military Flight Surgeon Pilots.

Let me pause for a moment on that last one—the International Association of Military Flight Surgeon Pilots. I want you to think about how much motivation, dedication, and determination it takes to become just a member of that elite organization, much less their President. The rigorous academics, the sleepless hours in the hospital emergency room, the night landings in his A-6 aboard an aircraft carrier that's sailing in the middle of an endless, pitch-black sea. You can't just throw words like doctor and pilot around. You must imagine the relentless drive that Dave felt inside—the drive that unfortunately left him to be, understandably so, the quintessential bachelor to Anne and Brenda.

But I guess I'm somewhat grateful he wasn't married because two nights before the launch Dave took me on a tour of the shuttle, perched on the launch pad, just itching to go fly. For the next two hours, we climbed every ladder, traversed every gantry, and said "hello" to just about every NASA technician that was readying the lady Columbia. It's during this tour that Dave stressed repeatedly to me that he was supremely confident in the maturity of the program. He was one hundred percent certain that every bolt, every wire, every checklist item was exactly as it should be. But most importantly, he was so very confident in those ordinary technicians that have extraordinary job descriptions—like Thermal Protection System Engineer and Space Shuttle Main Engine Technician. So, Mr. O'Keefe and Mr. Dittemore, as you both have said, and as Dave would certainly agree, let's figure out what went wrong, fix it, and get on with it. By the way, along with me and Dave were his two other Blue Team crewmates, Mike and his wife Sandy, and Willie and his wife Lani. Now you see why I was glad he wasn't married. Instead of that late night tour with the other spouses, I would've been back at the hotel watching "Joe Millionaire" or something.

So that almost says it all about our Dave Brown—Renaissance Man. But not quite, because Dave was also a fellow landlord to Jo Ellen M., a student to Jay S., a housemate to Janet P., Jim B., Charlie B., Brenda S. and Jane B., a best friend to Tom B., a member of the vestry to the Holy Trinity Episcopal Church congregation, a cousin to Paula M. and Nancy U., an uncle to Danny and Casey, a brother to Doug, a son to Paul and Dot, and a hero to millions like me.

Not a hero because of the manner of his passing, but rather because of the quality of his living. And today, I am here where we will lay my best friend's body to rest … on a quiet hillside … in a plot of land that overlooks a city of memorials … dedicated to thousands of other heroes … none of them quite like Dave.

ALL 8 CHECKLISTS

MAKE IT PURPOSEFUL

1. Audience scenario .... SELECT
    a. Inform the Industry
    b. Pitch the Prospect
    c. Compel the Customer
    d. Persuade the PM

NOTE

It's important to have one and only one of these scenarios in mind at a time. Changing the scenario will almost always require substantial revisions to an existing presentation design.

2. Sales cycle stages and purposes .... REVIEW
3. Preliminary PURPOSE .... SELECT

NOTE

Do not proceed any further until you have made this preliminary selection. Unlike the Scenario selection, you will have an opportunity to adjust prior to takeoff (e.g.,, rehearsal stage).

MAKE IT PERSONAL

1. SPIE .... PROFILE

NOTE

Use their social media, "About" pages on websites, curriculum vitae (C.V.), and official biographies (most VIPs will provide them in advance). You can also interview colleagues and assistants for clues. These same tools can and should also be used in item 4 of this checklist, Cater to the LEFT.

2. US vs. THEM .... SELECT A CONNECTION
3. US anecdote .... DESIGN

WARNING

Under no circumstances should you be disingenuous or design a flimsy connection ("Oh, wow, my 3rd cousin once removed grew up 150 miles from where you spent the summer before 9th grade"). This can immediately trigger the slimy-car-salesman-anaphylactic-shock response.

4. Cater to the LEFT .... GRAPH YOU AND THEM

Be sure to avoid behavioral conflicts such as an Egoist presenting to another Egoist. Be a Vincent.

5. Risk tolerance .... PROFILE
6. Speech Acts .... CHECK
   a. ASSERTIONS are true and sincere
   b. ASSESSMENTS are grounded by factual assertions
   c. DECLARATIONS are fully described

MAKE IT EMOTIONAL

1. DOSE your design .... CHECK
2. Insert relevant humor .... AS REQUIRED
3. Heuristic biases .... ETHICALLY MANIPULATE
4. Briefing schedule .... LAUNCH LAST OR FIRST

NOTE

If you are one of a series of speakers, because of the recency heuristic, it is best to go last in the series, if possible. The next best option is the pole position. If you "kill it" coming out of the gate, it's only natural for the listener(s) to look for faults made by the remaining presenters.

5. Speech Acts .... CHECK
   a. ASSERTIONS are true and sincere
   b. ASSESSMENTS are grounded by factual assertions
   c. DECLARATIONS are described by their vows

MAKE IT COMPELLING

1. Your customer's story .... PLOT THEIR PYRAMID

NOTE

There are two stories in every presentation: the story your listener has and your story. Use the blank form provided earlier to first diagnose your listener's story. If a company, search their website for clues: About, Press Releases, regulatory filings, etc. If it is an individual, use the same profiling TTPs mentioned earlier, but now from the perspective of the story they're living in.

2. Structure your presentation .... PLOT YOUR PYRAMID
3. Listener's existing moods .... RECEPTIVE OR RESISTIVE
4. If resistive .... DESIGN RECEPTIVE
5. Trust .... PROVE IT
    a. Engaged
    b. Able
    c. Reliable
    d. Sincere
6. Speech Acts .... CHECK
    a. ASSERTIONS are true and sincere
    b. ASSESSMENTS are grounded by factual assertions
    c. DECLARATIONS are fully described

MAKE IT VISUAL

1. Gather your data .... CHECK

WARNING

When requesting data from other colleagues, you can use fake data to help relay the narrative concept. Be sure to label it as fake. Be sure to review all slides for removal of fake data prior to final rehearsal.

NOTE

In gathering the data, you want to present, consider elements that will prove your trustworthiness (Engagement, Ability, Reliability, & Sincerity). Use SPIE to help chose US elements (e.g., using the same testing lab that your customer uses).

1. Images, charts, tables, others .... SELECT MOST APPROPRIATE
2. Slide Titles .... AVOID LOUVRE
3. Font typeface, size, color scheme .... SELECT
4. Sequencing .... VARIABLE

CAUTION

Intersperse graphical and textual slides such that there are no sequences of more than 3–4 of either type before switching.

6. Speech Acts .... CHECK
   a. ASSERTIONS are true and sincere
   b. ASSESSMENTS are grounded by factual assertions
   c. DECLARATIONS are fully described

MAKE AN OFFER CHECKLIST

While this is the shortest of the checklists, it is by far the most important.

MAKE AN OFFER (OR REQUEST)

1. Your purpose .... REVIEW AND ADJUST AS REQUIRED

During the design or rehearsal process of the presentation, the purpose originally intended from Step 1 may change. It is vital to review the purpose and opening slides and ensure the opening and closing thoughts are congruent.

2. Your offer/request .... CRAFT
3. Purpose and request / offer congruence .... CHECK

PREPARATION CHECKLISTS

PREPARE THE ENVIRONMENT

1. Determine optimum location .... SELECT

NOTE

When you have the choice of where to deliver the talk, know that specific locations send subtle psychological signals. Your site means more power for you and less for your customer. Vice versa if at their site. Refer to Step 7 for more information.

2. Seating layout for maximum interaction .... SET
3. Appropriate lighting .... SET

CAUTION

Ensure the lighting is bright enough for the audience to take written notes if appropriate, but not so bright that it washes out the screen or prevents you from seeing their faces. If able, turn down or out lights in the front of the room while keeping the back of the room well lit.

4. Clean and organized .... CHECK
5. Distracting ambient noise .... MITIGATED
6. Handouts .... CHECK

NOTE

Carefully consider your strategy for handouts. Beforehand and they might become a distraction as some listeners will want to thumb ahead. Waiting until the end may impact relevant notetaking ability.

7. Timing/scheduling .... FIRST or LAST

WARNING

For talks given as part of a sequence of many, choosing to be first is optimum since it will (a) catch the audience at their freshest state and (b) set the bar high for others. Going last is most memorable because of the recency bias.

PREPARE YOUR AUDIENCE

1. Mood .... ANTICIPATE
2. Authority gradient .... HIGHER
3. Attire .... DETERMINE NORM
4. Somatosensory engagement .... DEMO GEAR
5. Bio breaks .... SCHEDULED
6. Food / snack breaks .... SCHEDULED

PREPARE YOURSELF

1. Attire .... SLIGHTLY ABOVE NORM
2. Odors .... AVOID MALODOROUS

Avoid smoking, drinking, and foods that can cause foul odors.

3. Voice .... EXPRESSIVE
4. Facial expression .... TRUSTWORTHY
5. Posture .... CONFIDENT
6. Eye contact .... CONSTANT SCAN
7. Stage position .... SET
8. Pockets .... EMPTY
9. Pointer .... STOWED UNTIL REQUIRED

DEBRIEF CHECKLIST

DEBRIEF

1. Presenter's notes .... GATHERED
2. Observer's notes .... GATHERED
3. Audience surveys, if possible .... GATHERED
4. Any recordings, ... GATHERED
5. Goods .... LIST
6. Others .... LIST
7. If Declined, perform diagnostic .... SIN
    a. Situation
    b. Individual
    c. Narrative

OVERCOMING THE FORGETTING CURVE

Right now, I'm having amnesia and déjà vu at the same time. I think I've forgotten this before.

- Comedian Steven Wright

Throughout this book, I've made some promises regarding your expected outcomes:

- Enhance your presentation's impact and retention
- Reduce your fear and anxiety
- Increase your "yes" rate (listener's agreement to your issues, concerns, requests, etc.)
- Shift the listener away from distrust to trust

However, these outcomes are only possible if you take personal responsibility for your learning using the following tools.

In writing this book, I have anticipated Ebbinghaus' Forgetting Curve's influence. Therefore, I offer the following adult learning strategies for overcoming this natural forgetting tendency, remembered as the three Rs:

Repetition

Recursion

Reciprocation

REPETITION—USING A MASTERMIND MANDALA

Not only did Ebbinghaus study how quickly we forget, but he also explored the role that repetition plays in memory retention. One way to effectively review learning material is to revisit it frequently (daily to start with) until it becomes engrained in long-term memory. To support this process, I have created the Tell it Like a Topgun Mastermind Mandala™ for your use. Head over to the book's website to download https://tellitlikeatopgun.com/.

To use this tool most effectively, I highly recommend adopting Benjamin Franklin's "Thirteen Virtues" approach to overcoming the forgetting curve. At the ripe young age of twenty, Franklin was not satisfied with himself and recognized the need to establish a set of virtues that he should live up to. He created a list of thirteen and a mechanism for inculcating them into his persona, as he described in his autobiography:

> My intention being to acquire the habitude of all these virtues, I judged it would be well not to distract my attention by attempting the whole at once, but to fix on one of them at a time; and, when I should be master of that, then to proceed to another; and so on, till I should have gone through the thirteen.[99]

By using the mandala in a thirteen-virtues-like manner, focusing on one part of the mandala each week, you can significantly improve your long-term adoption of these practices.

For more on Franklin's method, visit http://www.thirteenvirtues.com/.

RECURSION—EXPLORING THE BIBLIOGRAPHY

I have made some bold claims throughout the book about our current understanding of the human condition and industry best practices to be successful in the design and delivery of oral presentations. Where appropriate, I have provided source material in footnotes planted on their relevant pages. While each of the references can be considered equally valid, as the adage goes, "Some are more equal than others." To become a more learned and practiced speaker, the following list of highly readable books is suggested as a starting point.

- *Conversations For Action and Collected Essays,* Flores, Dr. Fernando; CreateSpace; 2012.
- *Pitch Anything,* Klaff, Oren; McGraw-Hill; 2011.
- *Words that Work,* Luntz, Frank I.; Hyperion; 2007.
- *On Bullshit,* Frankfurt, Harry G.; Princeton University Press; 2005.

99 Franklin, B. (1909). *The Autobiography of Benjamin Franklin* (Vol. 41). PF Collier.

- *Sapiens: A Brief History of Humankind,* Yuval Noah Harari; Harper; 2015.
- *Thinking Fast and Slow,* Kahneman, Daniel; Farrar, Straus, and Giroux; 2013.
- *Behave: The biology of humans at our best and worst,* Sapolsky, R. M., Penguin Books. 2017.
- *The Visual Display of Quantitative Information,* Edward Tufte; 1983.
- *Envisioning Information,* Edward Tufte; 1990.

RECIPROCATION

This is the act of conversing with others who share the same set of distinctions. With the launch of this book, my team has created a portal (https://tellitlikeatopgun.com/) for readers to share their thoughts, lessons learned, and new reference material with each other. Please take advantage of the power of reciprocal learning.

You can also interact with me and my followers on the following platforms:

- LinkedIn: https://linkedin.com/in/jeffgoldfinger
- YouTube: https://youtube.com/@STEMSignal

We look forward to hearing from you.

ACKNOWLEDGMENTS

This being my third trimester of life, it is impossible to thank every one of my mentors, peers, friends, and family who helped me survive and thrive to this point. But I'll start by going back nearly 50 years to where I must acknowledge the contribution of my high school chemistry teacher. Dr. David A. Sousa yanked me from academic mediocrity and put me on a path that led to a Navy scholarship at Northwestern, a highly reputable school that allowed a disreputable character like me to graduate. While in college, my late Sensei Shojiro Sugiyama imparted the discipline and focus of the martial arts on my not yet fully formed pre-frontal cortex, the impact of which cannot be overstated.

My educational mentors, Dr. Fernando Flores and Toby Hecht, taught me the fundamentals of human nature and the philosophies of business, conversation, and care, and to have the courage to become a business owner. Todd Gautier, a fellow NSAWC instructor, as my boss in corporate America demonstrated the practical value of powerful business narratives and was the supportive springboard for my transition from the W-2 world to the freedom of owning my own training practice.

On the Navy side, I must acknowledge Captains "Rocco" Ersek, Dave Parks, and Brad Goetsch, for drafting me to serve under them at the three weapons schools (CAEWWS, NSWC, and NSAWC, respectively). It almost doesn't matter what else I have done in life, this book and my success as a public speaker would not have been possible without these crucial assignments. Observing the leadership speeches of CAPT(Ret) Dave "Roy" Rogers and VADM(Ret) Lyle "Ho Chi" Bien didn't hurt either.

Thank you Abbot Apter, Ron Kaufman, and John Christy, for the patience to read early drafts and the friendship to poke me in the eye about its flaws. Thank you to RADM(Ret) Bill Sizemore, and CDR(Ret) Dan Donoghue for your thorough read of the latter manuscript versions and effusive forewords. And, of course, Dr. Paul "Neuron" Zak, for checking me on my layman's translations of the academically dense neuroscience.

To my editor Patti M. Hall who was at once my coach, cheerleader, and commandant throughout this process. To Dino Marino Design for bringing forth the book's aesthetic vision from my 1s and 0s imagination. Ditto to MK at Deezign Depot for the TILT logo.

Extended duration gratitude to my decade-long Wednesday morning (Abbot, Brad, Dave, John, Ken, Melanie, and Susan) and 5-year long Friday night (Lampros, Mark, Mary Ann, Paula, Peter, Ron, Todd, and Tony) mastermind groups who were crucial to instilling the confidence and business acumen necessary to bring this book to life. To my brothers, Jim and Joel, who fully supported my Navy career, much to the chagrin of our mother. To my daughters Jami and Jacey for enduring a less than optimal childhood while I was pre-occupied with both my Navy volunteer "voluntold" duties.

Finally, to my son Abraham and wife Yeiry who, in the home stretch of this effort, encouraged me to push forward whenever I felt like stepping back.

Oh, and of course, to Doc, for a life well-lived and his spirit that's still alive inside me.

Made in the USA
Middletown, DE
16 January 2025

68515460R00146